Your
Man
ABEDNEGO

A play in four acts

By

Onyechi Mbamali

authorHOUSE®

AuthorHouse™ LLC
1663 Liberty Drive
Bloomington, IN 47403
www.authorhouse.com
Phone: 1-800-839-8640

Published by AuthorHouse   01/11/2012
First published November, 2010

ISBN: 978-1-4678-7772-5 (sc)
ISBN: 978-1-4678-7773-2 (e)

Printed in the United States of America

A candle light

for

a peerless pair

Akosa and Com Mbamali

(worthy parents)

CAST

Abednego ....Interpreter
Oyidi'a..Head wife of the demised king
Akaeze...Prime Minister

Dikeogu
Mmanko
Ajofia } Other high chiefs
Orimili Obiora

Ndukwe
Ifeka
Achi } Youth leaders
Odikpo
Egbuna

Oche-ilo-eze....................................Custodian of the king's square
Ebili ....Village drunk
Iwobi...Bed-ridden sick man

Obinna
Osita } Iwobi's sons
Umeji
Nnaeto

Mr Harvey J. Barnsley.....................District Officer, a white man
Rev. Jones...White Christian missionary
Ugochi...Orimili Obiora's wife
Nnenna ....Iwobi's third wife
Uzoma...Iwobi's daughter
Echezo...Palace staff
Hezekiah...A second interpreter

Two masquerades
4 unarmed policemen (one a lance corporal)
7 policemen armed with rifles (one a sergeant)
5 maidens with water pots (two of them, Ajofia's daughters)
10 youths, male
2 wives of Oche-ilo-eze
A handful of male and female layabouts

Mgbafor   a woman's apparition

ACT 1, SCENE 1

Here at the King's public square of Umudimkpa, it is dusk on the eve of the Mgbe Dike Festival. The atmosphere is charged with ogene beats and pulsating footfalls in the close vicinity. A camp fire burns in one corner as two youths chat in the foreground.

Achi: It is like the mystique of the *ogbu* tree: when you think they've killed it, it sprouts even stronger. This Mgbe Dike festival will be the greatest of all time.

Egbuna: I hear the footsteps and heartbeats. The great times are back. The immortals maintain their heartbeats in the footsteps of the braves.

Achi: Umudimkpa celebrates again the times of the heroes.

Egbuna: The *ogene* summons the living and the dead to a dance of destiny.

Achi: It will happen here in the public square.

Egbuna: Tomorrow is it. Tomorrow!

Achi: The whole world will hear Mgbe Dike, the commemoration of our heroes past and present.

Egbuna: For five long years, the land was gagged. We buried our heads in the shame and silence of collective cowardice. This kingdom could not celebrate Mgbe Dike because the white vomit at Ubulu ordered an end to our great festivals.

Achi: Forget the white dog. He put his face in the moon. But this land will yet swallow his head.

Egbuna: There is too much talk without action. How can the land shake when its people refuse to move their bodies? A stranger pisses on your feet and you do nothing. Who do you blame when he defecates on your head?

Achi: I tell you yet again, leave the white man alone. Let him puff as if there is no custom where he comes from. The gods of this land will teach him the same lesson that hot water taught the tortoise.

Egbuna: Umuachala did not wait for the gods. As soon as the white man showed the mischief in his hand, they fought him like men.

Achi: But they were massacred like fowls.

Egbuna: Better to die to the last man than accept shit eating a whole lifetime.

Achi: Better to be alive and witness Mgbe Dike again. My brother, there is victory in the patience of the elders. You and I will dance once more to the beat of *ogene*, the fervent escort of the braves.

Egbuna: I hear the succinct call. It is one with my spirit. Speak to me, *ogene*! I hear the iron-clad affirmation of your native truth.

Achi: I hear the instant code and bear witness. The cold blood of fear turns fire of daring spirit.

Egbuna: The ogene never plays for a coward.

Achi: Ogene never escorts a timid soul.

Egbuna   *[singing a decoding of the ogene beat]*:
           "Ejiro ogene edu onye ujo"
           The ogene has no part in the escort of a coward

Achi: *[chanting in response]*:
           Ejiro ogene edu onye ujo"

The ogene has no part in the escort of a coward

[Egbuna goes into an instant frenzy, breaks into a warrior dance]:

Egbuna: Ejiro Ogene edu onye ujo!

        [Achi quickly restrains himself, glances furtively]

Achi: Hold it, my friend. Contain it for now, contain it . . . The fine
            for infraction is a whole cow.

Egbuna   *[unrestrainable]*: Let the fine fall on my head! Whatever
            happens tonight, the blame should lie with the spirits.

Achi: Contain it, my man. Do not boil before you simmer. The
            simmering soup that boils over quenches the cooking fire.

        [Egbuna simmers down with a visible effort]

Egbuna *[now in a lowered voice]*:   "Ejiro ogene edu onye ujo!"

Achi *[looking over his shoulders, responds conspiratorially]*:
            "Ejiro ogene edu onye ujo"
            The ogene has no part in the escort of a coward

*[Exeunt, singing in subdued tunes, dance steps restrained. The ogene is
still playing. Enter Odikpo carrying a basket, Ifeka by his side]*

Odikpo *[heading to a corner]*: Over here, Ifeka. Give me a hand.

        [Ifeka assists in lowering the heavy basket]

Ifeka: Too much obsession with the white man's money. Who is
            going to buy all this stuff from you?

Odikpo: Listen to the ogene. Can't you hear what it is saying? *[singing]*
            "Ejiro ututu ama njo afia! Ejiro ututu ama njo afia!"

Ifeka: Is that what your ears are now telling you?

Odikpo: Ejiro ututu ama njo afia! Yes, the fortunes of a market day may not depend on the morning's outlook. It is very clear in my ears.

Ifeka: Human beings hear what they choose to hear.

Odikpo: And what is your own choice?

Ifeka: Is anyone in doubt about that? The raw sound of *ogene* brings out the warrior in me. I walk the path of our brave forefathers. I dare the mighty lion with bare hands, cut off a dozen heads on the battlefield and pass through the thorny forest unscathed. It is I, Ifeka, son of Ogbunife, the great one who kills in the open and walks in or out through the front door.

Odikpo: Unless the warrior in you can look the white man in the eye, except any of us can defy his iron laws and pull down his prison walls, all this talk of lion and forest takes nobody anywhere.

Ifeka: Hear yourself. You imagine that the white man is unstoppable? If he is the sky that never falls, why is he buckling? Why has he suddenly unbanned this festival? The gods of the land know where to squeeze a stubborn he-goat.

Odikpo: This particular he-goat overran the entire farm and nothing stopped him. We can celebrate all we care but who rules the land today? It is the white man and his money. If you don't have his money, you are useless in the new world.

Ifeka: When I hear this kind of talk, my head scatters like the oil bean. Must the sons of warriors become women—carry baskets of cocoyam and vegetable—for coins and cowries? Odikpo, you are my dearest friend, but this thing you are doing will split us like day and night.

Odikpo: You have no business mocking my business.

Ifeka: Your so-called business cheapens you before the eyes of common slaves. You are a true born, an offspring of warriors.

Odikpo: My father is languishing in the white man's prison. That's where the warrior thing landed him.

Ifeka: Your father made a bad mistake. He joined his mother's clan in their foolish decision to fight the white man in the open. That is Umuachala for you. Your father is lucky to survive at all. Countless others perished in that blunder.

Odikpo: So, let us learn. It is futile to challenge fate. The only person in this whole world who does not recognize his superior is a dead body.

Ifeka: The white man is not our superior. He is only a seasonal blight, like a pimple on a damsel's face. Umudimkpa has chosen the right way to deal with it. You have to be involved.

Odikpo: It's a long vigil tonight. People may need my supplies. If I make some money, what is anybody's problem with that?

Ifeka: This is Mgbe Dike festival. I won't let you spoil my mood. I got myself a brand new bullhorn. It is rearing and tearing to summon the valiant from their ant holes.

Odikpo: You know the hefty fine if that thing sounds even once. Oche-ilo-eze, keeper of the king's public square has not performed the opening rites. He is not even showing any hurry to make his invocations. So your bull horn must wait.

Ifeka: It will wait in quiet dignity. But stop provoking us with washer words.

Odikpo: Nobody hears from me all night except they want to buy my stuff. I am your silent pal as long as my basket is secure in this place.

[Odikpo stows his basket away in the shadows. Ifeka paces, fiddling with his bullhorn]

Ifeka: The night is heaving, ready to break out. It is like a score of live pythons in a sewn jute sack.

Odikpo: The heat will pass. Isn't that what *chinchi*, the bed bug assured her young ones?

Ifeka: This is a different kind of heat. It is burning my nerves and searing my very heart. It is fever! How can we get the old man to feel the excitement and start us off?

[Enter Oche-ilo-eze, gaunt old man leaning on a tall staff]

Oche-ilo-eze: The old man is never moved by excitement; only by the gods. That is why he is still keeping the king's public square.

Ifeka and Odikpo *[surprised]*: Oche-ilo-eze!

Oche-ilo-eze: Yes it is I, Oche-ilo-eze. All my age have gone into the ground. But I'm still here, in charge of these grounds. Both of you—run and join the chase out there. One of my tethered rams has broken loose. I want it back, on the quick.

[Ifeka and Odikpo scamper away. Re-enter Achi with a high stool which he positions in the corner]

Oche-ilo-eze: I did not request for a chair.

Achi: The aged must not be kept standing.

Oche-ilo-eze: The aged should not be robbed of choice or deceived by pretences. It is only when you young men need something from an old man that you show any respect.

Achi: Oche-ilo-eze, it is not only the young that want you to commence the celebrations. The whole kingdom is waiting for you as keeper of the king's public square.

Oche-ilo-eze: Run along, young man. Join your mates in the chase of the fleeing ram.

Achi: It has been caught, already, Oche-ilo-eze. And it is now bound with a stronger rope. You can hear it bleating, awaiting a death sentence from you.

Oche-ilo-eze: Nobody alive tells me when to invite the spirits to dance on these grounds.

Achi: It is your prerogative, Oche-ilo-eze.

Oche-ilo-eze: My family's place from generation to generation. I gauge the mood and character of creatures—especially those you cannot see with human eyes. They are legion, but I only permit entry to benign beings. Otherwise evil forces will overrun the palace and the country. Most of you think it is a child's play.

Achi: Anyone who thinks so should have his head examined.

[Re-enter Egbuna, Odikpo and Ifeka, with five other youths, some bearing low stools]

Oche-ilo-eze: Most of your age mates should have their heads examined.

[The youths position their stools opposite the high stool]

7

Egbuna: Why is the blame always on the youths? What about the
             fumbling elders, Oche-ilo-eze?

[His mates begin to hush him but Oche-ilo-eze stops the noise]

Achi: Please don't talk like that to Oche-ilo-eze.

Oche-ilo-eze: Let him talk. The future belongs to those who ask the
             right questions. Speak on, young man.

Egbuna: Oche-ilo-eze, why do you elders so fear the white man you
             won't let us fight back? The youths of Umudimkpa are ready
             to give him the fight of his life. We can put him on a non-stop
             ride to oblivion. Why do you stop us every which way?

*[More youths arrive, more low stools and a big calabash of palm wine.
Oche-ilo-eze halts another wave of noises.]*

Oche-ilo-eze: Those who rush to fight the white man with machetes
             and spears are empty in the head. They only bring woe
             upon their own necks. Every dog has his night. It takes wary
             walking to see the light of dawn.

Egbuna: The white man is a long dark night in this place. When do
             we arise like true sons of warriors and chase him back to his
             own country?

Ifeka: Mgbe Dike is what we are here to mark.

Egbuna: Mgbe Dike is only a celebration and it is just for four days.
             After that, what happens?

Ifeka: Let's first finish with it. We haven't even started.

Achi: Starting depends on Oche-ilo-eze when he hears the spirits.

Egbuna: How come the white man himself has no regard, even for the spirits? And why do the spirits seem powerless to stop him?

Oche-ilo-eze: Hear that one. It wearies me that you young people know nothing at all. Do you really think the white man just woke up one morning, smiled at the sky and rescinded his ban of our festival? Your generation is too glib, too shallow. You put your heads in the clouds when only an ear to the ground can hear the lyrics of the ants.

[Still more arrivals]

Egbuna: We are getting crowded. Why don't we let Oche-ilo-eze take his seat?

Achi: Don't interrupt his flow. Do we hear such opportune wisdom every day?

Egbuna: There is more wisdom in sitting down to hear!

Oche-ilo-eze: Ah! The young men of nowadays! They cannot bear standing for even a short while. It is such a shame. You are much too spoilt, much too spoilt! At my age, I can still stand all through the night.

Achi: That is an uncommon power, Oche-ilo-eze. The immortals that gave it to you did not give it to everybody.

Oche-ilo-eze: You are right in saying that. Perhaps I should indulge you a little tonight. All right, all right. Let's all sit down.

All: As Oche-ilo-eze pleases.

[Several willing hands assist, busy doing little, as the old man sits. Then all sit in a half moon before him—some on low stools and logs of wood, others on the ground]

9

Oche-ilo-eze: The thrills and throbs of masquerade tunes may capture the night; the whole earth may be fired up, but Oche-ilo-eze remains indifferent to the things that excite mortals. Until I sound my ancestral *ekwe* to release the Mgbe Dike spirit, not a grain of dust here will respond to all that clamour raging out there.

Ifeka [*rising to his feet*]:   Oche-ilo-eze, you are the ageless custodian of this park and the whole kingdom respects the powers the gods conferred upon you. The Osilike Age Grade here with you tonight has tied a ram to your door post to announce our new masquerade coming out tomorrow. That ram is yours, horns and hooves.

Achi: The white man urinated on our shrines. We have taken a decision to wash away the evil by a special libation this night. You will pour it for us with the most expensive hot drink in the white man's country.

Ifeka: This Age Grade handed Odikpo the full money to purchase that powerful gin. [*Lowering his voice.*] All the way from Onicha, the big trading post.

Odikpo: It is here.

[*Odikpo hands over a bottle of gin (J.J.W. Peters) and Achi lays it at the old man's feet*]

Oche-ilo-eze: Is it the one they call '*nje-nje*'?

Achi: That very one, Oche-ilo-eze. It is a drink for strong heads only.

Egbuna: The aroma alone can get a passerby drunk.

Ifeka: That is very true, Oche-ilo-eze. We also delivered some other presents which will speak for themselves at your doorsteps.

Oche-ilo-eze: I did not ask you for presents, did I? *[A pause]* Anyway, as father to all of you, I should not reject your goodwill. *[A longer pause.]* But we must wait for the gods. Only they will tell us when to commence the rites.

Ifeka: The gods should feel our anxiety. It's been five years of silence.

Egbuna: Five years of a pregnancy that mocked the manhood of the kingdom. The entire Osilike are dying to sound the ant holes. The deities should feel our pains and heartbeats.

Achi: Hear the *ogene* frenzy. It is now a rage around the square—a blasting fire storm. Are the gods still not impressed?

[The ogene sounds reach a crescendo]

Egbuna: Oche-ilo-eze, your eyes have seen everything in life. You are the grand patron this age grade looks up to. What can we do now to induce the gods?

Oche-ilo-eze: You are on duty with me tonight, young men. It is not to induce the mighty ones but to listen out to them for the whole kingdom . . . But if your ears are already full of *ogene* rush and rampage, what can you hear but common rivalry, the premature dance that cripples infant antelopes? What is that to the gods?

Ifeka: Please permit us to confer awhile, Oche-ilo-eze.

[Ifeka signals to Achi & Egbuna and all three step aside and confer]

Ifeka: This approach is not working. Let's stop trying to rush him.

Achi: You are right. We were warned against arguing with him.

Egbuna: How else can we get him to begin?

Ifeka: Let's be patient. A bully can never hold up a child's plaything for ever; an eventual cramp will force down the raised hand. Let's just relax and let the old man run his show.

Achi: I concur.

Egbuna: As far as he doesn't spend the whole night mouthing empty air.

[They regain their places]

Ifeka *[standing]:*   Oche-ilo-eze, I salute you again on behalf of the Osilike Age Grade. We apologise for that eagerness of youth that often seems to put the wrong foot forward. Osilike will sit in quiet at your feet and hear your wise counsel.

Oche-ilo-eze: The young readily dance away all the common sense they need to face the future. That is why I agreed with the palace that before the gong beats of ceremony lend you flighty wings, I must drill some reserves of sense into your ears. *[A pause.]*

Ifeka: You have our attention, Oche-ilo-eze.

Oche-ilo-eze: How many of you have been to the white man's trade post?

Egbuna: We don't want to even know the road to that place.

1ˢᵗ Youth: They say it is a journey of many days.

Achi: Odikpo is the only one of us that goes there.

Ifeka: We allow his trips, the only exception. He has to see his father who has been moved there from the Ubulu prison.

Egbuna: But he has started misusing the opportunity. He now trades. And he thinks we haven't noticed.

Achi: That should not be our business.

Egbuna: It is our business because one finger that contacts grease will
            stain the rest. These things happen small by small.

Ifeka: Oche-ilo-eze, we are as firm as all our senior age grades on
            this matter. Osilike refuses to have anything to do with the
            white man's trade posts.

Oche-ilo-eze: The same mistake.

Ifeka: What mistake, Oche-ilo-eze?

Oche-ilo-eze: It is the folly of every generation to drift in their shift.
            Where is your sense of mission and the drive to reach it?

Egbuna: The only mission that counts is to stop the white man. Our
            total boycott of his trade post is proof we mean business.

Oche-ilo-eze *[laughing mirthlessly]*:   Hear that one. Talking about
            meaning business, do you understand the meaning of
            business? Time's eternal mischief is to hide wisdom from
            youth till old age overtakes their own power to use it. What
            is your quarrel with the white man's trade post?

Ifeka: We are only following the example of our seniors, the
            decision taken from the onset by all Umudimkpa. Is that a
            bad thing now?

Egbuna: Blame is a must that is reserved for the youths. If we lie
            down, it is indolence; if we get up, it is disobedience.

Oche-ilo-eze: Blame your confusion on your own forwardness, young
            man. You take the wrong paths in life because you never ask
            those ahead of you what they have seen or what they are
            looking for. You have no ears for experience, so you repeat
            common mistakes.

Egbuna: I don't get this at all. Are we being told to now become friends with the white man?

Oche-ilo-eze: I am giving you the benefit of counsel and you better hear it. You cannot defeat the white man by keeping away from him. How would you know the secret of his power or the things that cook for him? We don't even know where he comes from that his skin is such a strange colour.

Egbuna: Why do we need to know all that? The only thing to figure out is how to chase him back to wherever he emerged from. Mgbe Dike is our finest opportunity if the gods will fight on our side.

Oche-ilo-eze: The oracles are quite definite on the matter of the white man. He is not going to be chased away as quickly as you wish.

Ifeka: That is no good news.

Oche-ilo-eze: But that is the naked truth. He is going to be with us for a very long time.

Egbuna: Is that the way the gods want it or we have failed the warrior spirit of our ancestors?

Oche-ilo-eze: Whatever grain you pick for yourself, none of us can defeat the white man today. The only thing we can do is to persuade the roots and leaves of this land to make the soil of Umudimkpa unwelcome to him. Let him prefer Ubulu and never settle on this land.

Egbuna: He has already taken Ubulu without a fight. Now, he is getting stronger and stronger and we are just watching. What is the fate of this kingdom?

[A pained silence]

Oche-ilo-eze: If we want to uproot the white man from all his bases and trade posts, we must know what he knows.

Achi: He knows too many things that he may not tell anyone.

Ifeka: We should ask the gods to expose his secrets.

Oche-ilo-eze: Why bother the distant gods? You have one among you who is a traveler. That is the person to ask.

Ifeka: Odikpo should speak for the gods?

Egbuna: Is it this Odikpo or another one?

Oche-ilo-eze: The home-grown palm fruit is often despised in the quest for oil.

Egbuna: But a palm-fruit does not run more oil than its mates by a visit to the market.

Oche-ilo-eze: Hear me, young men; whoever travels afar sees afar like the spirits themselves. If indeed you want to know any important thing about these new times, you must hear from the mouth of the traveler in your midst.

Egbuna: What is Odikpo's interest except the selling price of market stuff?

Achi: You are always picking on Odikpo. Did he eat your seed yam?

Ifeka: Odikpo, you heard Oche-ilo-eze. Tell Osilike, the secret of the white man's power if you know it.

Odikpo *[rising to his feet]*: Grandfather Oche-ilo-eze, I greet you. And I greet my brothers, the Osilike.

All: We greet you too.

Odikpo: The white man writes things against you in a book, so he never forgets anything. His people open the book and straight there, they see everything and you cannot deny. That is power.

All: It is magic. Real juju.

Egbuna: We can burn his book with fire if that is all.

Odikpo: It is not all. The white man's biggest power is his money.

Egbuna: I knew he would come to that.

Odikpo: Maybe it is not the money itself but the clever way the white man has hidden it in the very open. You see the money with your eyes. But you can never get a bit of it unless you work like a beast or sell everything you have to him. If you steal it or kill for it, he puts you in his prison and you cannot escape.

Egbuna: Let us call the truth by its name and stop this dancing around a whole forest. It is the prison that is the white man's strong house. If we cannot rise and burn it down, we are no different than the inmates.

Achi: Ubulu is not the only prison. There are several other prisons in various places. We even hear of a new big one they have built in Onicha. How many are you going to burn down?

Ifeka: The white man is not a tame beast to be wrestled with bare hands.

Achi: That is why we must find out his secrets. Without a good battle plan, we cannot even scratch his skin.

Ifeka: Odikpo, tell us more of the white man's secrets.

Odikpo: What is there to add to what I said before? Oche-ilo-eze, the white man's power is his book and the money. Even so, the secret of the money is hidden in the book. So, whoever has the book will rule the new world.

[Odikpo regains his seat in the remote corner]

Oche-ilo-eze *[contemplatively]*:   I hear in those few words, the weighty wisdom of a true traveler. Young men, you too have heard. But I don't know if the words just entered one ear and passed out through the other. I need you to confirm with your own mouths that you heard what I heard.

All: We heard well, Oche-ilo-eze.

Oche-ilo-eze: What I can espy from my ground seat here as an old man, you may never sight it from the treetop as youngsters. *[Rises to his feet, crouched against his long staff]* If I was young like you, I would not be looking for a prison to burn. The prisons are needful. That's where we shall put away the white man some day for what he is doing to our lives.

[Oche-ilo-eze begins to move away, very slowly, not forgetting to pick up the bottle of gin. All rise to follow him]

Ifeka: Put the white man in his own prison? Is it possible, Oche-ilo-eze?

Oche-ilo-eze: Every dog has his night, my boy. But you need power—the power in the white man's book to know his secrets. Then, it is up to you to chase him back to his own country! Or you hold him in the prison he built for us.

Ifeka: Oche-ilo-eze, the strangest thing is that the whites are so few in number. I can count them on my fingers in the whole region. How can so few subdue so many?

Oche-ilo-eze: It's all there in the white man's book. His best kept secret is how he divides kindred and turns brother against brother.

Our fellow blacks now kill for him and speak for him—as if there is no life without the white man.

Ifeka: There is one new fellow, the bearded one who speaks our very dialect, yet no one knows where he comes from.

Achi: The one they call Abadi . . . Abadi-something . . . I forget. Odikpo, please remind us of his name.

Odikpo: Abadinegwo!

Egbuna: That man is a thief!

Ifeka: He is even worse than the fat one, the one that fell sick and died.

Egbuna: All of them are thieves. But this new one is the worst ever! Seven goats and ten pots of oil, that's what he took on his first appearance!

Achi: But who can tell if he is stealing for himself or for his master? He jaws and echoes for the white man because he has the power of his language.

Oche-ilo-eze: All that power is in the book. Gain it for yourself, Osilike. Then Umudimkpa shall be strong to deal with any alien masquerade.

[Exeunt all but two anonymous youths]

1st Youth: In fact, that Abadinegwu is a masquerade!

2nd Youth: A big bushy beard covers his face, like overgrown weeds.

1st Youth: His head is always bandaged.

2nd Youth: Why does he wear a hat on top of the bandage?

1st Youth: His right eye hides behind a strange glasss. That is what I don't understand. Why does he wear that thing?

2nd Youth: They say he is blind in that eye. Someone said that thieves broke his eye some years ago.

1st Youth: Thieves? Is he not one of them?

2nd Youth: He's a very strange man.

1st Youth: A real masquerade—that's what he is!

[Fade]

ACT 1, SCENE 2

Morning next day, at the king's public square of Umudimkpa. Four barefooted, baton-wielding police constables in starched khaki uniforms march onto stage in single file. Leading from behind, the fourth man (a lance corporal by the oversized, single stripe on his left sleeve) regulates the march with his whistle, finally bringing movement to a stop with a long, shrill blast as they get to the centre. He steps aside, blows the whistle sharply and bawls out orders.

Lance Corporal:	'Tention!
	Tandaatiz!
	Righ' tua!
	'Tandaatiz!
	'Tandizzy!
	[surveys the premises with distaste.]
	Very bad at all. Where them?

Constable 1:   I think their men are hiding.

Constable 2:   No, they have gone home after last night. Until about noon, you will only sight their women.

Constable 1:   Foolish people! No fight if we want to finish them.

Constable 2:   Fear these people. They are more dangerous asleep than awake.

Lance Corporal: Order!

All: Yes sah!

Lance Corporal: Their power finish.

All: Yes sah!

Lance Corporal: White man power, no challenge!

All: Yes sah!

Lance Corporal: 'Tention!

All: Sah!

Lance Corporal: Who are we?

All: We are police!

Lance Corporal: Police power?

All: Gorment power!

Lance Corporal: Who no know?

All: He go know!

Lance Corporal: White man power?

All: No challenge!

Lance Corporal: Any complain?

All: No complain!

Lance Corporal: 'Tandaatiz!

All: Sah!

Lance Corporal: 'Tandizzy!

All: Yes sah!

Constable 3:   What go do now?

Lance Corporal: We wait white master, yes . . . and Oga Abadinegwo, yes.
                They greeting palace finish, they meet us here, yes!.

Constable 2:   The Square is empty until noon, then masquerades will fill this place. Who is the white master coming to preach to?

Lance Corporal: What is your chair inside? Very bad at all! Order!

All: Yes sah!

Lance Corporal: Rev. Jones and D.O. them white brothers, yes! If wind or water he want or preach to sand or stone, he carry go.

All: Yes sah!

Lance Corporal: Carry how?

All: Carry go!

Lance Corporal: Very good at all!

Constable 3:   But...there is too much dust here, Corp'l. White master will not like it.

Lance Corporal: That is true, yes. Very bad at all! What go do now?

Constable 1:   We can get water and wet the ground.

Lance Corporal: That is correct, yes. Quick, quick. Order! Arrest water!

[The three constables head in different directions, but a shrill blast of the Lance Corporal's whistle halts them]

Lance Corporal: Very bad at all! You want die? Order! We move together!

All: Yes sah!

Lance Corporal: Two you go there, two we go this side.

All: Yes sah!

Lance Corporal: These people very dangerous. We stay together!

All: Yes sah!

Lance Corporal: So two-two we go!

All: Yes sah!

[Exeunt in separate pairs. Enter Ebili, large calabash in hand]

Ebili: The arrogance of strangers who won't respond to greetings
            makes me laugh. See them badgering women for
            water—women who are returning from the stream!

*[Glimpses of maidens, each with her water pot balanced on her head,
hurrying away from the obtrusive constables. Some giggle flirtatiously,
some seem terrified but none is yielding]*

            Which maiden will give you water in the midst of Mgbe
            Dike? Only the one agreeing to marry you . . . It is not by
            force; no, no, it can never be by force. See, you don't accost a
            girl on the village path as if she has no home. No, you wait,
            like a well-bred son of a decent family. She approaches her
            parent's compound, and then you step up and ask for her
            water. The water is her own. Who is your father to take it by
            force?

*[The constables are beginning to look frustrated at their lack of success.
The girls wiggle away, seductive-looking in their scant native attire]*

            Not the whole pot! Aah, ah, never the whole pot—just
            enough to drink or rinse your mouth or wash hands and
            feet. And you must ask nicely. Not gruffly like ruffians. What
            nonsense! Do you think you can intimidate a daughter of

Umudimkpa? Aha, because you are wearing fancy cloth? Fancy cloth you borrowed from the white man? Aha, or because you march like this—like waddling ducks coming out of a pond. *[Mimics a parade march]* Ebili, many things are happening before your very eyes in this land. It is the stuff of good laughter! *[Peers into his calabash]* Is there still a drop in this calabash *[shakes the calabash close to his ear and listens, then takes a swig]*

Let me tell you something if you care to know. A daughter of Umudimkpa will rather break her water pot than let a stranger grab it. And this is Mgbe Dike time. Ha! If any pot breaks—okokoko! Trouble will grow mustache!

[Re-enter the Lance Corporal, looking frantic. With a shrill blast of his whistle, he summons his men back to the square. Ebili in the far corner, sits unnoticed on a log. He drinks from his calabash, shakes his head to clear it and watches]

Lance Corporal: Very bad at all. Why the no water? Why?

Constable 1:   The girls are refusing.

Lance Corporal: Order! Not refusing. You look them bobby! Why look them bobby?

1st Constable: Me no look, Corp'l

2nd Constable: Me no look at all.

Lance Corporal: You look, all of you! I see with eye. Order!

All: Yes sah!

Lance Corporal: Very bad at all. No water. Why?

Constable 2:   True, Corp'l, these women don't obey.

Lance Corporal:	Order! Why begging? We arrest! Who are we?
All:	We are police!
Lance Corporal:	Police power?
All:	Gorment power!
Lance Corporal:	Who no know?
All:	He go know!
Lance Corporal:	White man power?
All:	No challenge!
Lance Corporal:	You three go, I stay. No beg. Arrest.
All:	Yes sah!
Lance Corporal:	No more look woman bobby!
All:	Yes sah!
Lance Corporal:	How many pots?
Constable 2:	Ten.
Constable 1:	No, twenty!
Constable 3:	We wet only white man corner.
Lance Corporal:	Order! Twenty pots!
All:	Yes sah!
Lance Corporal:	Go! Twenty pots! Arrest!

All: Yes sah!

*[The three troop out. Ebili hovers a few metres away.
Lance Corporal observes him]*

Lance Corporal *[truculently]*: What do you want here?

Ebili: Who questions the other—the passing wind or the sitting land?

Lance Corporal: Order!

Ebili *[laughs aloud]*: That's what you always shout. Odour! What does it mean?

Lance Corporal: Very bad at all! You are drunk. Why drunk in early morning?

Ebili: *[drawing close]*: Drunk is better than stupid. What's your own choice?

Lance Corporal *[shrinks away]*: Order!

Ebili *[shaking with laughter]*: Odour! That's what you always shout. Odour! Then your men say: 'Ye-ssah!'

[Fade]

ACT 1, SCENE 3

Throne Room at Umudimkpa palace. Four high chiefs (Akaeze, Dikeogu, Mmanko and Orimili) are seated with Oyidi'a. Except the now middle-aged Obiora who replaced his father as Orimili when he died some ten years ago, all are very old and feeble. Eto'odike is bed-ridden and no longer attends meetings in the palace. The Ebekuo stool vacated four years back by the death of the last holder is the subject of a fierce contest which should be soon resolved now that the colonial administration has lifted the ban on native festivals.

Dikeogu: What exactly does the white man want this time?

Akaeze: We shall hear when he arrives. I'm only following the *ekwe* beats which the watch has been posting since early morning. Other than that, there was no prior word of this visit.

Dikeogu: I hope he is not coming to impose another tax on our heads.

Mmanko: Did our festival kill his mother?

Dikeogu: The same question I asked the open sky this morning. It is really getting very annoying. What can we do to remove the eye of the white man from our body?

Akaeze: When we see his face, we shall hear from his mouth. Remember, it is not their head man at Ubulu that is coming.

Mmanko: The *ekwe* says it is the bearded one.

Akaeze: Yes, the one who tells us to close our eyes to pray.

Dikeogu: All white men look the same to me. The same long noses. They all sound like humming birds.

Mmanko   How do they understand themselves? I can never know.

Dikeogu   Don't evil birds understand themselves?

Oyidi'a: The praying one is not an evil bird. We hear amazing reports how he goes about attending to sick people and giving help to everyone.

Dikeogu: I fear that type of kindness from a total stranger.

Mmanko: It is a trap. It must be a trap.

Dikeogu: Truly, I understand a stranger who comes to fight me. But any who comes smiling at me like an eager bride, I wonder what he wants.

Akaeze: Are these ones still strangers? They have settled in to stay, all around us. The one that is coming is even asking for land in this very kingdom. He wants to build his house of worship here.

Dikeogu: As we agreed last time, a portion of the evil forest should be given to him and his kinsmen.

Mmanko: That is the place for them. Free, very free!

Akaeze: I am happy that the festival has not precipitated any death or fight; so no one is coming to fault us here.

Dikeogu: I find nothing to cheer at all. Just look at us—high chiefs of this great kingdom. We sit here, waiting for an alien who has reduced us to common bystanders in our own land. The white man decides who breathes or who walks on the road. I should have died than seen this time.

Orimili Obiora: You will not die, Dikeogu. The battle of machetes and spears may be over. But the battle of the brains is only just beginning. This land needs its finest warriors at this awkward time. You are one of the very best.

Dikeogu: Orimili Obiora, you have taken your great father's place in the grace of office and the worth of words. I wish I left like him in the glory of high noon.

Akaeze: The gods are kind to deny you that wish. Everybody will not quit the fight of life in the same breath. There must be surviving elders to hold the torch of wisdom or the land will consume itself.

Dikeogu: It is a fate I bear with open grief, to count my closing days in this sorry fashion. When a dreaded masquerade overstays its outing, it becomes a village clown.

Oyidi'a: Dikeogu, is it not strange how you allow the weight of years to sit on your head? Look at Akaeze who is older. If we weren't here to stop him, he would even marry a new wife.

[General laughter]

Akaeze: You are not the ones stopping me, Oyidi'a. I am only waiting for the white man to bring me one of his sisters.

[More laughter]

Dikeogu: Just advise your white in-law to leave us in peace. His visit should not kill us; neither will his departure give him a hunch back.

Mmanko: Does the white man understand a proverb?

Dikeogu: Does he feed through the nose? He must have some brains or why are we here breaking our big heads for a glimpse of his little smile?

Orimili Obiora: I know this may sound absurd; but I no longer consider the white man as our real problem. Our fellow blacks are the ones beating the drums for him. A masquerade can only dance as good as the drumming that escorts him.

Akaeze: You are right, Orimili Obiora. It is the house rat that informed the field rat that there is fish in the smoked basket.

Orimili Obiora: Every secret of our kingdom is in the closed fist of the white man. That is what I find very disturbing. He reads us like the lines on the palm of his own hand.

Dikeogu: The fault is our own for looking good at a stupid cost. Will the sky above fall on us if we seize the opportunity of this festival to do what needs be done? I think it is time. We should do something for our pride as a people.

Mmanko: Dikeogu has spoken my mind!

Oyidi'a: We must resist the urge to rush into another direct confrontation. Let's not forget the heavy fines that always follow. Our restraint and patient wait is already yielding fruit.

Dikeogu: Oyidi'a, the fruit before my eyes is a rotten one. Mgbe Dike should ask the ancient questions.

Mmanko: That is how it used to be. The oath of blood and a few human heads . . . . then, the land is sober again.

Oyidi'a: What about Umuachala? They moved to appease their land in the ancient way. What happened instead?

Akaeze: We are living witnesses, all of us.

Orimili Obiora: Their own land gave them up for slaughter by the white man. Men and women were cut down like rabbits.

Oyidi'a: Will they ever recover from that carnage?

Orimili Obiora: There is no family in the whole land that is not still grieving over that calamity. Umuachala are our cousins

Oyidia: Their pain is our pain. But what befell them is an abiding lesson to every clan. To me, the path we have chosen here is the path of wisdom.

Akaeze: It is the dreadful fate of Umuachala that settled our own arguments of months in this very palace. We cannot afford to repeat their mistake. Mgbe Dike will ask the ancient questions but only with the blood of rams.

Mmanko: Ajofia warned us yet again. He has complained often and often that the gods are not happy with animal blood that we are forcing down their throats. Is it good to ignore the words of the Chief Priest as we are doing? It is not good.

Akaeze: This is a closed matter. We stopped the spilling of human blood in this land well ahead of the white man's coming.

Orimili Obiora: My father told me about the tough debates. Posterity will honour this council for giving standing legs to Igwe's foresight.

Dikeogu: Those are sweet words. But nobody is telling me how we can remove the white man's eye from our body. Who appointed him the guardian spirit to oversee our compounds and save us from our own soup pots?

Akaeze: We must walk the long path of patience together. Except we remain steadfast, we may never find the door of hope.

Orimili Obiora: The trouble is our fellow blacks who behave like foreign goats in their own place of birth.

[Enter Oche-ilo-eze, stoops low before the vacant throne]

Oche-ilo-eze: Igwe! Long may you live. Akaeze, Oyidi'a, noble high chiefs, the King's Square salutes the Throne.

31

All: Oche-ilo-eze!

Akaeze: Is all well that you bring yourself?

Oche-ilo-eze: The land will never run away, but a few strangers have chosen to test Umudimkpa this morning. What they did was done on the king's square; so I have to come in person. Igwe and his high chiefs should hear direct from my lips.

Akaeze: The palace never denies a ready ear to Oche-ilo-eze. A strong house is only as safe as its premises.

Oche-ilo-eze: You will pardon my heavy lips, Akaeze, for the questions filling my mouth.

Akaeze: Let us hear them.

Oche-ilo-eze: Someone is asking if this is still Mgbe Dike, the appointed time to celebrate the legendary valour of this kingdom. I was asked if it is still that special week when the menfolk make proof of their power as warriors. A fellow asked me whether this is no longer that ordained time when our children and womenfolk feel the full assurance of our protection and love. I came over to ask because five daughters of Umudimkpa are crying like orphans at my door.

Oyidi'a: What happened to them?

Oche-ilo-eze: They were returning from the stream when four bastards beset them and broke their water pots!

[Shocked exclamations]

Akaeze: Spirit or mortal, who did this?

Oche-ilo-eze: Pigs who speak the white man's language and fly his cloth in our face.

Mmanko [*on his feet*]:   What does the white man want from us? His servants molest our women. Why are we sitting here waiting to receive him like a king? I am going to my house.

Akaeze: If that is the hiding place of the vandals, run quickly and capture them for us.

[Mmanko retakes his seat, chastised]

Dikeogu: Mgbe Dike of our forefathers! Umudimkpa of our greatness! What is happening to our pride?

Orimili Obiora: It is very frustrating. No matter how much a man strives to avoid a touch of trouble, the loose ends of his robes may drag it all to him.

Dikeogu: Trouble is like a mound of shit at your doorstep. It is self-deceit when you fail to remove it and you prefer stepping around it. How long can you do that?

Oche-ilo-eze: I need Igwe's quick decision. We must take precautions or the machetes of family honour will flood the fields with sudden blood.

Oyidi'a: Whose daughters are they?

Oche-ilo-eze: Ajofia's youngest daughters and their three friends.

[Gasps from various persons]

Mmanko: Ajofia!

Oyidi'a: Akaeze, this one is big trouble.

Akaeze: It doesn't come any worse.

[Fade]

ACT 1, SCENE 4

The King's public square at Umudimkpa. A white clergyman, Rev. Jones in white soutane and black shoes preaches to a scanty crowd of natives. Abednego, a heavily bearded middle-aged black man, wearing a monocle and a rimmed hat, a white short-sleeved shirt and baggy brown khaki short knickers and black sandals, interprets.

Rev. Jones: In those days,

Abednego: In the days of Doz, the great one,

Rev. Jones: It came to pass—

Abednego: It rushed in to rush away—

Rev. Jones: —that men were falling short of divine expectation.

Abednego: Short men were falling. It was not expected.

Rev. Jones: There was a great longing to know God.

Abednego: Everybody began to get very tall to near God.

Rev. Jones: People were longing.

Abednego: People were growing tall.

Rev. Jones: They were longing.

Abednego: They were growing very tall.

Rev. Jones: They were longing to see God.

Abednego: They grew very tall to see God.

Rev. Jones: There was a great multitude.

Abednego: There was a powerful masquerade.

Rev. Jones: All the way from Tyre to Siddon.

Abednego: On all long roads where you tire, you sit down.

Rev. Jones: They were looking for a prophet.

Abednego: What they wanted was profit.

Rev. Jones: A prophet to declare heaven's will for mankind.

Abednego: Profit to clear the well in heaven for kind man.

Rev. Jones: He warned them against mischief.

Abednego: He made them one against Miss Chief, the chief's daughter.

Rev. Jones: He stood in their midst as I stand in your midst today

Abednego: He stood and they missed as I stand, you will miss today

Rev. Jones: He addressed the multitudes

Abednego: He undressed the masquerades

Rev. Jones: In the same way today, I address you as a multitude

Abednego: In that same way today, I will undress your masquerade

Rev. Jones: His very proclamation I repeat to you today:

Abednego: His own porcupine (that wicked animal) I release on you today:

Rev. Jones: Eschew evil and mellow down.

Abednego: Chew a bad thing well and swallow it down.

Rev. Jones: Love one another

Abednego: He-enh?

Rev. Jones: Love one another

Abednego: Love one person first, later love another

Rev. Jones: Don't be selfish

Abednego: Don't be selling fish; only meat is allowed.

Rev. Jones: Eschew murder and needless conflicts

Abednego: Yes, chew your mother with needles and corn flakes

Rev. Jones: Stop back-biting

Abednego: Stop biting people on the back.

Rev. Jones: Henceforth

Abednego: The hens fought. *[Aside]* Chai! White man loves big, fat chickens.

Rev. Jones: Let there be peace

Abednego: Allow people to piss

Rev. Jones: The axe is under the tree

Abednego: Ask them under the tree

Rev. Jones: If you are a thief, woe betide you

Abednego: If you be thief, Iwobi tied you

Rev. Jones: If you're a murderer, woe betide you

Abednego: If you are your mother's area, Iwobi tied you

Rev. Jones: If you do violence, woe betide you

Abednego: If you do anything that has no meaning in our language, Iwobi tied you

Ebili [interrupts, stepping forward]:   How can Iwobi tie anybody? Which Iwobi?

Abednego: What?

Ebili: Iwobi tied nobody. He has been on sick bed since last year when he fell off the palm tree.

Abednego: Shut your mouth. How dare you talk when the white man is talking?

Ebili: Tell white man that Iwobi cannot tie anybody. The man cannot even move arm or leg to tie anyone or untie himself.

Abednego: Foolish drunkard, you don't know spiritual talk. Have you never heard that the white man is a spirit?

Rev. Jones [to Abednego]:   What is he saying?

Abednego: He is drunkard from village. Palm wine scatter his brains. He talk nonsense.

Rev. Jones: What a pity.

Abednego: Not Apiti. This one is Ebili.

Rev. Jones: I mean . . . uh . . . It's a pity.

Abednego: No, this is Ebili, not Apiti.

Rev. Jones: Uh . . . never mind. Tell him that drunkenness is an evil sport of the devil. It ruins lives and sends a soul to hell.

Abednego: The white man is a spirit. *[To Ebili]* Did I not warn you? He says the devil has finished you and you are dying. You will go straight to hell fire.

Rev. Jones: But there is good news for you, my friend, if you can only believe. Yes, believe and be delivered today.

Abednego: Chai! This man is finished. Today, today your liver will die. Even that one is good news. This man is finished!

[Ebili is looking at him quizzically]

Ebili: You sound like someone. I can't remember whom. But you sound very familiar.

Apiti: I don't know you and you don't know me. You are drunk as always. Go away now or I command police, they put you in prison!

Rev. Jones: What are you saying to him?

Abednego: He said bad, bad thing. Now he begging you money. He want buy that strong drink—that strong gin of white people. He say bad, bad thing.

Rev. Jones: What did he say?

Abednego: He say you'self drink hide your mouth. I tell him that is wicked lie.

Rev. Jones: Well, that's not a lie. I was a drunk myself but the Lord delivered me.

Abednego: Your own liver?

Rev. Jones: Not liver. Deliver. That means: set free. The Lord set me free.

Abednego: Oho.

Ebili: I feel I know you and I think I don't know you. And I know you think it doesn't matter if I know you since you don't know me.

Abednego: Get away from my face!

Ebili *[Drifting back to his place]:* If nobody knows me, my calabash still knows me and I still know my calabash. And I know what is inside it. That's enough to know. Why know someone who doesn't know me?

Rev. Jones: Poor fellow. I've been there in that pit. I know that feeling of despair and utter rejection.

Abednego: Did you hear that, you drunkard? White man says you are poor-follow. You will be poor and follow poor people. Next time you talk when white man is talking, your tongue is rejection. Whether you are drunk or mad, watch yourself from now on.

Ebili: I will never watch anything but my calabash. I can live without my tongue. Kill me; it's a pot of meat. Sell me; it's a bag of money.

[Reactions from the sparse crowd are mixed and muted. There is a nervous stir—a bit of consternation and some awkward laughs]

Abednego: What can be worse than madness or drunkenness?

Ebili: Echoing the white man's foolishness! That's what.

[Concerned voices urge restraint from Ebili but he rebuffs all]

1st Plebeian: Ebili, be careful what you say!

Ebili: They are telling us Iwobi tied people! Which Iwobi?

2nd Plebeian: I was surprised too. Iwobi is paralysed from head to feet.

1st Plebeian: He is my neighbour. I know how bad he is suffering.

Ebili: How can he tie anybody?

Fat woman: Be careful how you vouch for anybody. You don't know who is using witchcraft in the night.

1st Plebeian: That is very true . . . . Iwobi's first wife comes from Amame, the headquarters of witches.

Fat woman: The white man is a spirit. He cannot lie.

Rev. Jones: What are they saying?

Abednego: They talk Iwobi—that winch who tied everybody. He fall down from palm tree.

Rev. Jones: Is a man dead?

Abednego: Die he no die, live he no live. Just lie there, like dry bush meat.

Rev. Jones: My heart goes out to him.

Abednego: White man is a spirit! You people, hear this. White man said his heart will fly out like a powerful bat, to fight that man. It is going to be a battle of witch and spirit!

Ebili: That is not the fight we are waiting to see.

Abednego: What other fight do you want, you drunkard?

Ebili: Mgbe Dike masks are on their way to this place. There were five broken water pots this morning. Umudimkpa will ask you a few questions.

Abednego: Are you out of your mind? Are you going to question the white man?

Ebili: No. If White man puts a curse on his head, it doesn't concern us because we don't hear his Espli-spli-spli! It is you that we heard the words from because you are the one who echoed forbidden things on your own head. Didn't you boast here in public that you will undress masquerades and we the people shall all miss? The masks are coming. We are waiting to see who will undress whom.

Rev. Jones: What is he saying?

Abednego: He talk say juju is coming. Why you no respect juju?

Rev. Jones: Juju? I suppose you are referring to the festival masks. That's a sport, a mere circus.

Abednego: Not circles and not one spot. Mgbedike go everywhere with matchet very wicked. Cut somebody head, religion, no prison.

Rev. Jones: That's not religion. That is savagery and the law will deal with that. Tell these people that true religion is love. Tell them our mission here—how we tend the sick, feed the poor, help the helpless and bring humanity to the light of God.

[The ogene beats and chants are heard approaching. Abednego is listening with a bit of apprehension]

Abednego: Where police? They must come now, now.

Rev. Jones: I've ordered the police back to Ubulu.

Abednego: Ah! Ya! Ya! big mistake! I tell you no do. Why you do?

Rev. Jones: They had no right to molest these people. I am here to preach the gospel of peace. Tell them what I told you to tell them. Gospel of peace.

[The chant is now discernible:]

"Ogene, Ogene	Ogene, Ogene
Mmanwu de!	The masked spirit salutes
Ogene, Ogene	Ogene, Ogene
Mmanwu de!	The masked spirit salutes
Anyi g'etizi ogene	Shall we play ogene
mmanwu esoro anyi o	with no masked spirit
Mmanwu de!	The masked spirit salutes
Anyi g'etizi ogene	Shall we play ogene
mmanwu esoro anyi o	with no masked spirit
Mmanwu de!	The masked spirit salutes
Okokoko!	O what a grief!
Mmanwu de	The masked spirit salutes
O k'osi adi o	That's how it goes
Mmanwu de!"	The masked spirit salutes

Rev. Jones: You haven't interpreted that. Gospel of peace.

Abednego: Piss! Me self, I want go piss now, now.

Rev. Jones: Well, quick with it, please. Why is everyone getting nervous?

Abednego: Neighbours?

Rev. Jones: Nervous. Fear. What are they afraid of?

Abednego: They fear before say Iwobi is winch. Now they fear say mask be coming this place. Mask be dead people spirit you talk say you undress it.

42

Rev. Jones: Undress? I said no such thing!

Abednego: Oho! *[Aside]* Aha! Tortoise is clever in denial, Squirrel smarter in escape.

Rev. Jones: What did you say?

Abednego: I say I not afraid. I come back quick, quick. I first hurry go. Piss.

[Exit Abednego. The ogene beat and chant intensify with approaching footfalls. "Ogene, ogene, mmanwu de!" Rev. Jones regards the small crowd of a dozen before him. He opens a big wooden box and displays some bright coloured towels and white singlets]

Rev. Jones: Come. *[The people watch, not comprehending. He begins to signal to them in a friendly way.]* Come. Come. *[Holds out a towel to them]* Take . . .
Somebody take.

[Some hesitancy in the little crowd . . . A few tentative steps by a handful end in abrupt recoil, to a staccato of nervous laughter. Rev. Jones grabs a couple of towels and goes to them, handing out to those willing to collect them. He keeps repeating: "Take . . . Take. Say 'Thank you'. Take. Say 'Thank you.'" as he moves round. Some shrink back, but after an initial reluctance, three or four persons accept the gift and begin to admire it]

Rev. Jones *[flushed with excitement and beaming with smiles]*: Say 'Thank you' everybody. What is 'Thank you' in Ibo? I suppose it is 'daalu'. Say 'daalu'. Daalu!

Crowd *[surprised and amused]:* Daalu. Daalu.

Rev. Jones: Daalu nu.

Crowd *[appreciating his effort to speak their language but amused at his accent and poor pronunciation]:* Daalu.

[A rampaging Ogene troupe led by Ndukwe bursts onto stage and the crowd scatters instantly, leaving only Ebili who keeps a safe distance]

Ndukwe/Ogene Troupe *[alternating]*:

> Ogene, Ogene
> Mmanwu de!
> Ogene, Ogene
> Mmanwu de!
> Anyi g'etizi ogene mmanwu esoro anyi o
> Mmanwu de!
> Anyi g'etizi ogene mmanwu esoro anyi o
> Mmanwu de!
> Okokoko!
> Mmanwu de!
> O k'osi adi o
> Mmanwu de!"

[The chanting youths charge in all directions, stomping the ground and brandishing menacing cudgels. They are fierce-looking, bare-chested and gleaming with sweat, their raffia skirts flying as they streak here and there in wild runs. Rev. Jones stands watching, his face expressionless. The troupe converge, dance in dusty circles, then turn to face him.]

Ndukwe: This is white man. He does not hear language, neither does he know masquerade. Who will tell him for me that white or black, no mortal strives with a spirit for right of way? . . . . Who will advise him to go home to his mother before an evil wind carries him to a distant place of no return? Somebody please warn him that the coming masquerade is not a friend of strangers. *[He intones another song and his men supply a throaty chorus—"* Imago mmuo di ifaa?*" ["Do you know the identity of this very spirit?"]*

> *[in alternation with his troupe]*:

> Okoko, Okoko saa iyoo
> Imago mmuo di ifaa?

Okoko, Okoko saa iyoo
Imago mmuo di ifaa?
Akataka nya na agu gbalu mgba
Imago mmuo di ifaa?
Otokilika ka obu
Imago mmuo di ifaa?
Eziokwu, otokilika ka obu
Imago mmuo di ifaa?

"Okoko, Okoko respond
Okoko, Okoko respond
Daredevil that tangled with the leopard
A veritable monster is he
Indeed, a real monster is he!"

[Jangling bells and a blaring bull horn usher in a grotesque and ferocious masquerade. It is armed with a mean-looking matchet and there is a restraining leash on its waist—a long rope pulled by three sweat-covered young men who themselves are in obvious terror of the rampaging brute. Matchet raised, it charges towards Rev. Jones, but the minders pull it back whereupon it turns upon them in great fury. They flee, dropping the rope momentarily, but quickly race back and regain it as it lunges again at the immobile Rev. Jones.]

Ndukwe: Restrain, restrain . . . but for how long? Who will tell the white man for me that stupidity is not courage? A rabbit that stares a lion in the eye—that is his last encounter. The smell of laity is offensive to ancestral spirits. Who will interpret to white man for me? The blood of strangers may not be sweet on the shrine of discretion; but it runs cheap on the path of stubbornness. Who will advise this one to turn quickly now and go back the way he came?

[He intones the next song and his troupe chorus animatedly]

Ndukwe/Chorus *[the troupe repeating each line after him, the bell now jangling ominously]*

45

Onye isi ike pua n'uzo
Maka mmanwu anyi egbue mmadu
Onye ogbulu onaa n'iyi
Onye isi ike, pua n'uzo
Maka mmanwu anyi egbue mmadu
Onye ogbulu onaa n'iyi
Onye isi ike pua n'uzo
Maka mmanwu anyi egbue mmadu
Onye ogbulu onaa n'iyi

"Stubborn fellow, off the way
Lest our masquerade will kill someone
Whoever he kills ends as nothing."

[Rev. Jones stands staring fixedly. The big masquerade suddenly breaks loose from its minders. It races forward, then begins a slow menacing prowl towards the white preacher, its jangling bell lending a funereal heaviness to the ogene rhythm and endless chant . . . . Fade.]

ACT 1, SCENE 5

The King's public Square at Umudimkpa. Rev. Jones sits on his wooden box, a large Bible open on his lap, under an improvised shade in the noon-time heat. He is down to white fatigues, his soutane hanging on the make-shift tent. Oche-ilo-eze and Orimili Obiora are locked in a spirited argument with Ndukwe, the Gosiora troupe leader, his five sullen mates standing with cudgels behind him.

Oche-ilo-eze: The gods are kind to Umudimkpa. But for their mighty hand that drew me here, these ignorants would have set the whole country on fire.

Ndukwe: We are the Gosiora Age Grade, Orimili Obiora. It is our immediate juniors, the Osilike who are coming to prime at this festival. We are not small boys. The white man must show respect or die.

Oche-ilo-eze: You can hear for yourself the garbage in their mouths. Are they small boys? No, they are not. But they would scatter the world like small boys to show that they are not small boys.

Ndukwe: It is the white man who wants to scatter the world, not us. But we must put a leash on his madness. No mortal is allowed to stand in the way of our masquerade in the manner he has done! Anyone who cares for this man should advise him to back off or his head will roll in the dust.

[He brandishes a matchet but his mates restrain him. Rev. Jones maintains a detached air, leafing quietly through his bible]

Orimili Obiora: Does the man understand a single word of what you are saying?

Ndukwe: That is his own headache. Orimili Obiora, this man is on our own soil. Why should we allow him to despise us with such impunity?

Orimili Obiora: I am looking at his long beard. It tells me that he comes from a very far place, a journey of many days or even months or years. We don't know the ways of his people. He himself does not know the ways of our masquerade.

Ndukwe: So, we teach him in a way he will never forget.

Orimili Obiora: He may be the masquerade of his own people. What are you going to teach a masquerade when you are only a man? Leave him to the gods. That is the wisdom of the elders.

Ndukwe: It is a hard thing, Orimili. Is there no man left among us?

Orimili Obiora: It takes real men to forbear costly fights. Tell all Gosiora that this one is not your own battle. It is a showdown of masquerades and there is no need for matchets.

[Enter Ajofia, bare-chested, chalk marks on his body and one eye encircled with white paint. He looks grim in a shin-length plain red wrapper, a palm-frond piece clamped between his teeth, a rod in one hand, a fly-whisk in the other, multiple feathers sticking out of his red skull cap, and a goat-skin bag slung across his shoulder. Two sullen-looking girls walk in silence before him, dressed in a two-piece calico that covers their budding breasts and hips. The trio acknowledges nobody's presence and returns none of the several greetings. The girls halt and point at a spot close to Rev. Jones and Ajofia goes there. He gesticulates with them for confirmation, goes down on his haunches with visible effort and three times, scoops a fistful of soil which he presents to the sun and empties into a gourd from his goat skin bag. He looks up again at the sun, then gets up with effort. Exeunt Ajofia and his female pair, wordless]

Oche-ilo-eze: Even a deaf knows the outbreak of war. There is no need for words.

Orimili Obiora: Is it not as we told you? This is a battle to be fought up there! It will blaze by itself where talk is expensive!

Ndukwe: I hear your words, Orimili Obiora. The sound is sweet in the ear, the substance even sweeter in the heart. Gosiora is now reassured. We can see that at long last, the mystical powers of the kingdom are about to be let loose.

Orimili Obiora: The sappling that stands on the path of the hurricane can only curse its own stars.

Ndukwe: Let things begin to happen to this stranger and any others like him who do not know how to stay or when to leave.

[Ebili steps forward, calabash in hand]

Ebili: That man is not bothered by curses. He is the proverbial tough beast that grazes in the open fields even under a hail of gunfire.

Orimili Obiora: Ebili, my good friend, you sound like his juju man.

Ebili: What juju does he need? He already has clearance from the gods as Oche-ilo-eze did not stop him. So it is these young men of Gosiora that I just don't understand. If their masquerade was smart to retreat, it means the spirit has left. What use is human argument when the spirit has gone away?

Ndukwe: Our duty is to clear the square for our juniors. Hear them coming, the hotheads of Osilike. Does anyone think they will accept a mess of their day without a bloody fight?

[Ogene rush of the Osilike Age Grade is heard].

Oche-ilo-eze *[pushing two of the young men]*: Move that log here. Yes, that one. And this one . . . . and that one too! Bring it here.

[Under his direction, a cordon is improvised for Rev Jones' occupied area as the Osilike chant intensifies]

49

Caller/Chorus *[alternately]*:

> *Osilike!*
> *Anyi abia!*
> *Osilike!*
> *Anyi abia!*
> *Osilike!*
> *Anyi ejee muchata mma, anyi abia!*
> *Osilike!*
> *Anyi abia!*
> *Osilike!*
> *Anyi abia!*
> *Osilike!*
> *Anyi ejee muchata mma, anyi abia!*

> "When the going gets tough
> We'll be there
> When the going gets tough
> We'll be there
> When the going gets really tough
> We sharpen matchets and get right there"

Ebili *[with a sudden spark]:*   Orimili Obiora! Do you hear what I hear? The pods of melody are bursting in my veins. Is it the same for you? *[Tentative dance steps]* Ah, it is again like yesterday! Yes, the years dissolve, calling up every bit of me. The memory of our own time covers my cap with eagle feathers. I feel like heading to the sky. Orimili, are you left behind? I am airborne on the transport of the spirits!

Orimili Obiora: It is the magic of *ogene,* my brother. But we must plant our feet firmly on our duty post or be taken by a dance of death.

[The Osilike troupe bursts on stage, led by Egbuna. All are armed with cudgels except Egbuna who wields a metal spear festooned with bright coloured cloth strips. He leaps and prowls and drives the spear into the ground.]

Egbuna/Chorus *[alternating]*:

> Osilike!
> Anyi abia!
> Osilike!
> Anyi abia!
> Osilike!
> Anyi ejee, muchata mma, anyi abia!

Egbuna: Osilike *dei dei dei!*

Chorus: Yaa!

Egbuna: The eye that sees an eagle must pause to celebrate
For the eagle is not an everyday spectacle
I see the brightness of title and plumage
The fullness of my mouth offers due greetings
Orimili Obiora, Endless River that Follows His Own Course
Osilike presents self before you in salute
Oche-ilo-eze, Guardian of the King's Premises
It is your mandate we brandish for passage
Osilike *dei dei dei!*

Chorus: Yaa!

Egbuna: Gosiora, you walked this path, then assured us
There is nothing to fear but much to gain in the covered basket
It was your brotherly love that informed us
Of a ripening berry in the thick of the forest
If by chance, we pluck it ahead of you
You will eat the reserve portion of our noon promise
Osilike *dei dei dei!*

Chorus: Yaa!

[The Gosiora troupe confer very briefly]

51

Ndukwe: Gosiora will now yield space to his junior brother.
            The glory of seniority is a worthy successor
            On hunting day we shall regroup as one
            A market day reserved, smoking with cheery praise
            On the trail of grass-cutter we shall all converge.
            Gosiora *dei dei dei!*

Chorus: Yaa!

[Gosiora men cross sticks with their Osilike counterparts in salute as warriors. Exeunt all Gosiora]

Egbuna/Chorus *[alternating]*:

        Osilike, gwam ife anyi na acho
        Onwelu onye anyi na acho
        Osilike, gwam ife anyi na acho
        Onwelu onye anyi na acho
        Osilike, onye ka obu anyi acho?
        Oke mmanwu ka obu, okpal'ike n'oge gboo;
                oke mmanwu k'obu
        Osilike, onye ka obu anyi n'ekwu?
        Oke mmanwu k'obu; okpal'ike n'oge gboo;
                oke mmanwu k'obu
        Osilike, onye ka obu anyi ga afu?
        Oke mmanwu ka obu; okpal'ike n'oge gboo;
                oke mmanwu k'obu

        "Osilike, tell me what we're looking for
        There's someone we're looking for
        Osilike, tell me what we're looking for
        There's someone we're looking for
        Osilike, who is it we're looking for ?
        A great masquerade he is;
        valiant in ancient times, a great masquerade!
        Osilike, who is it we're talking about?
        A great masquerade he is;
        valiant in ancient times, a great masquerade!

Osilike, who is it we shall see?
A great masquerade he is;
valiant in ancient times, a great masquerade!"

Egbuna: Osilike *dei dei dei!*

Chorus: Yaa!

Egbuna: Hmm! Hmmm!
I sniff in the air the foul smell of laity. Hmm!
Is it the father of albinos or a person of white body?
Curses fill my mouth, anger roasting my heart
My warring hand trembles for the grip of a matchet
Osilike *dei dei dei!*

Chorus: Yaa!

Orimili Obiora: Voice of the brave that called my name in praise
Am I allowed the privilege of an interjection?

Egbuna: The partridge may partake of the broadcast rights
His father is joint owner of the forest
Osilike that gave me voice gives ear as well to notables
Orimili outweighs soup and soup pot
Osilike is wise in thirsting for his words!

Orimili Obiora: Osilike, I greet you.

Chorus: Orimili!

Orimili Obiora: I greet as well what drums for you and what dances for you.

Chorus: We greet you too.

Orimili Obiora: The palace conveys a hefty basket of regards to Osilike. We know what *ogene* does to the blood of warriors, more so in the first dance of full manhood. But the times are

53

drawing our ears to caution; so every grown-up is invited to understand that stampede may be folly, that every dance is not war, and a sheathed matchet does not imply cowardice. Osilike, anyone home?

Chorus: We are legion, Orimili.

Orimili Obiora: In a season of wicked provocations, the valiant is tested for patience; yet the bravest warriors attest in all the ages that Restraint is ever the last man standing. The valour that is Umudimkpa forbids excesses; and villainy shall always be an outcast in these parts. The eye should never be scratched as severely as it itches; the finger that refuses restraint would deliver blindness. I speak to you as fellow men, not pretenders whose only claim to manhood is a joystick between the thighs. Osilike, anyone home?

Chorus: We are legion, Orimili.

Orimili Obiora: One who kills for the fury must bury for the stench. Osilike, are you still there?

Chorus: We hear you, Orimili.

Orimili Obiora: In the days of yore, when the open sky was playground for the squirrel, and the field yam knew very well the hand that planted it, no high chief would stand here spraying words like this. But colours of life are changing before our eyes, and wisdom must wear a blended complexion. What you see behind me is the new colour of provocation. But I stand here with Oche-ilo-eze to tell you to ignore it completely. There is no show that sucks blood from the eye. Osilike, anyone home?

Chorus *[half-hearted]*: Orimili . . .

Egbuna: I don't get this, Orimili. Are you saying . . . . wait, is that person going to remain here? Remain on these grounds when our masquerade arrives? *[Tearfully]* No, no, no! Seniors, this is not fair. You cannot do this to us.

Orimili Obiora: Listen, young fellow. Egbuna, listen to us.

Egbuna: No! Osilike will not be made a butt of jokes for the sake of useless peace! We refuse to be a laughing stock!

Orimili Obiora: Nobody will be a laughing stock. Hear me out!

Egbuna: This is too much, Orimili. We have told you elders, leave the people of white body to us. We know what to do and they will go looking for themselves where they can never be found. It takes us nothing to throw this one and his big box out of this place. How can we let him take our grounds on the very day of our masquerade?

Ebili *[aside]*:   The man is not even bothered at all. He doesn't even notice the flying words. White man is a spirit! Tough beast that grazes in the open fields despite a hail of gunfire!

Orimili Obiora: The battle is not yours, Egbuna.

Egbuna: This battle is mine and mine is the battle. My two sisters were molested this morning. Water pots broken at Mgbe Dike! Does anyone imagine there are no men in my family? I know the meaning of my father's silence.

Oche-ilo-eze: You know nothing. Your father Ajofia is Chief Priest of the whole kingdom. He is not saying anything because he knows what you don't know. This very fight belongs to the gods who will surely fight it for Umudimkpa.

Ebili: See, the man you are discussing is neither moved nor moving—he is like a piece of land in dispute. If any of us could speak his language, maybe he would shake a bit. But his interpreter has gone like smoke. I like to speak his funny language. Espli—spli-spliiiii, espli! Espliii!

Egbuna: Nobody will confuse us on this one. We shall never give place to a vulture!

Orimili Obiora: What you have just called him is his right name, Vulture! The ugly bird that every community must put up with! Who is Vulture, my good friends? He is a bird that never mourns the dead. But ages ago in another country, it was a different story one day when he observed that the last of the remaining elders were dying off in the community. It bothered him that young people were uninformed about his status and might sooner mistake him for common meat and start aiming all kinds of stones and kid slings at him. So, he summoned an emergency meeting of all the surviving seniors; it was there they resolved to let all youths know for all time, that vulture flesh is no food for humans. Osilike, are you home?

Chorus: Orimili . . . .

Orimili Obiora: Regard that person over there as the vulture of our time. For now, ignore him. And I mean, ignore him! The rest of this arena is space enough for all you want to do. When a luscious udala fruit falls near a smelly mound, wisdom will pluck a broad cocoyam leaf to cover the mound and pick up the fruit.

Ebili: It is not even a matter for many words. Unfortunately, young people drag when they should dig.

Egbuna: Ebili, this matter did not invite your calabash!

Ebili: True, but if Oche-ilo-eze allows a vulture to perch on these grounds, it means the gods allow it; so let it perch. The elders know how to fix a vulture. Have you forgotten that proverb about vulture eaters? Once they form their quorum, the smoked basket will come down!

Oche-ilo-eze: That saying is for real men, not infants who bathe only their belly when taking a bath.

Ebili: Something must happen before our very eyes—if people don't hurry to break their own legs like baby antelopes.

Orimili Obiora: Ebili is right on that matter, my friends. Dance your dance of youth by all means, but leave the nodding of heads to the watching elders.

[Enter Ifeka, bullhorn in hand]

Ifeka: Why the long quiet? What silenced the ogene? What is going on?

[Egbuna yanks up his staff and steps aside for a brief chat with Ifeka who soon signals their mates to join them. They quickly confer, then Egbuna returns, drives the staff into the ground again and roars]

Egbuna: Osilike *dei dei dei!*

Chorus: Yaa!

Ifeka *[to the seniors]:* Osilike will not refuse the counsel of elders.
A son should never wrestle his father for the
Drink horn of wisdom to keep as a trophy.
A young man shuts his eyes with grit
Or he cannot swallow a testy lump with grace.
Osilike salutes the day and night of elders *dei dei dei!*

Chorus: Yaa!

Orimili Obiora: The honour returns to Osilike. Day and Night will serve you.

Chorus: Ise-e!

Orimili Obiora: Oche-ilo-eze, please add your blessing. Then we can
            leave them to their big day.

[Oche-ilo-eze bends to the ground, scoops a handful of dust, mutters into it, looks up and throws it into the air]

Oche-ilo-eze: He that pounds well pounds in the mortar
            He that pounds silly pounds on the empty floor
            Osilike has decided in true manhood, and
            I bear witness
            Whoever goes averse, O soil, hunt him down.

Chorus: Ise-e!

            [Exeunt Orimili Obiora and Oche-ilo-eze]

Ifeka: Osilike *dei dei dei!*

Chorus: Yaa!

Egbuna: The master hunter's heart is bursting with fury.
            The hunt tickles and tempts with an imminent kill.
            One stroke of the matchet, it's a settled thrill.
            Is it friend or foe who asked me to be still?
            Lament of wood-pecker is for his swollen bill.
            Osilike *dei dei dei!*

Chorus: Yaa!

Ifeka: The path of a hunter is the path of war.
            Every step on the ground must be measured sure
            And the sky above must be courted close.
            A prey could turn predator, so to prey you pray.
            The quarry that mocks restraint is quickest to meet death.
            Osilike *dei dei dei!*

Chorus: Yaa!

Egbuna: Though the sword is sheathed, plain drink may be death;
Traps and snares are broken, yet rabbit may not roam:
Common smoke is fatal, let bush rat be warned!
Casting wicked spells, that's what they proscribed,
Who can prevent airwaves that cause the head to spin?
Osilike *dei dei dei!*

Chorus: Yaa!

Ifeka: The bull horn a trembling is fever in my hand
Summons of the mighty I feel and I must go
Back to my vigil post by the stirring ant hole
Leave me not stranded in cold and silent wait
Blast off the ogene, embolden your herald
Osilike, my brothers, I greet you one more time!

Chorus: We greet you too!

Egbuna: Let the ogene report! Let it be quick and sharp
To cut the sleep of ages and rouse even the lame
Lend even the tortoise the pride of stomping feet
To dance a dance of power like a raging bull
A wake of elephants in the next stampede!
Osilike gather my greetings!

Chorus: Yaa!

[Ifeka gives a sharp solitary blast of his bullhorn. Exit]

Egbuna/Chorus *[alternately, and to strong beat of ogene]*:

    Osilike, onye akpakwana agu aka n'odu
    Onye akpakwana agu aka n'odu
    M'odi ndu, m'onwu l'anwu
    Onye akpakwana agu aka n'odu
    Osilike, onye akpakwana agu aka n'odu

Onye akpakwana agu aka n'odu
M'odi ndu, m'onwu l'anwu
Onye akpakwana agu aka n'odu

"Osilike, let no one try the leopard's tail
Let no one try the leopard's tail
Alive or dead, a leopard
Let no one touch the leopard's tail"

[Lights dim. Fade.]

ACT 1, SCENE 6

Late night at the King's Square. Ebili is sitting on a log in the corner, playing soulful tunes on his flute. Rev. Jones in soutane, is kneeling in prayer beside his tent in the soft glow of a log fire.

Ebili [*flute play, with intermittent voice-over*]:

> Madness is fun to watch
> But no one wants it in the family
> Here's a stranger, is he mad?
> Or just abandoned by his own
> Or he abandoned his very own?
> Who can tell, let him tell.
>
> What is he doing here?
> Away from all comfort
> Away from those he knows
> Who know his meats and moods
> What fun or find he seeks with us?
> Who can tell, let him tell.
>
> All day long no food, no drink
> In blazing sun whose joy is it
> The furious blasts, ogene fever
> The rabid dust peppering the eye
> The wracking sneezes and running nose?
> Who can tell, let him tell.
>
> Night time is here, what more unfolds?
> A banquet for mosquitoes
> Or red beef for night flies
> A ready meal for night dogs
> Or night chop for bats and owls?
> Who can tell, let him tell.

Ebili gathers his scattered thoughts
Child of deep waters picks up his calabash
Sad to leave the stranger to himself
The path to sanity is a straight walk home
Crowd or crew, whose cry is it up-creek?
Who can tell? Who can tell?

[*Exit Ebili. The soft light gets dimmer. Rev. Jones, sneezing from time to time, rounds up his prayer and steps to the forecourt. He points his bible to the sky with his right hand. The light brightens a little.*]

Rev. Jones: Tonight O Lord, I stand in this place. In this moment of quiet after the day-long din, I claim this community for the glory of your name. May your word be fulfilled as it is written: 'a people that sat in darkness have seen a great light.' I thank you for choosing a lowly vessel like me for this mission at this time. Prosper your work, O Lord and one day, this very place on which I stand will house a chapel to your eternal praise. Amen.

[*Enter four hooded men. They encircle Rev. Jones and quickly wrestle him to the ground. He is only able to shout "Jesus! Jesus!" They gag him, pull his soutane over his face and truss him up with a rope, tying his wrists to his ankles behind him*]

2nd man: We've done it! We've really done it!

3rd man: I never believed we could tie white man.

1st man: I told you people. He's a human thing like us.

3rd man: Let us carry that box. It is his power.

4th man: No, we must not touch anything else.

1st man: What we have done is enough to show him that hot water can kill tortoise! Let's get out of here!

[Exeunt. Rev. Jones is left on the ground, grunting at intervals and straining without success against the binding ropes.] [Blackout.]

ACT 2, SCENE 1

Throne room at Umudimkpa palace. Akaeze and Oyidi'a converse, standing near the entrance.

Oyidi'a: So it is true?

Akaeze: It is pure madness. Whoever did it does not wish this kingdom well at all.

Oyidi'a: What is Oche-ilo-eze saying?

Akaeze: What can he tell us that won't amount to lame excuses? Where did he keep his eyes? I am going to question the leaders of those two age grades by myself. I have sent for them. They must tell us who tied the white man with a rope.

Oyidi'a: We must hear from Ajofia as well.

[Akaeze takes his seat. Oyidi'a follows suit]

Akaeze: Ajofia is not an infant. He will not puke in open watch. All eyes are on him and he knows the implications of a silly tantrum.

Oyidi'a: There is a report that he was there before noon yesterday. He collected soil in the full view of many people. They say he spoke no words but you and I know Ajofia. He is clearly up to a big revenge.

Akaeze: We cannot prevent him if he sends spirits to fight. Any of us who has the know-how is free to do as much. It is all right to invoke the soil and sky of Umudimkpa to defend her sons and daughters. The white man and his insolent agents should be taught their limits. Anything that can be sent against them is all right provided it is not of human stock.

Oyidi'a: I agree with that, Akaeze. A community must never cause its people to turn out as the living and smell like the dead.

Akaeze: Oyidi'a, what we are facing in this present age is an evil war that is stronger than human heads. So, whatever spiritual prowess we put to use is fair. The white man at Ubulu can put people in his prison; let's see how he copes with forces that his eyes cannot see!

Oyidi'a: I wish our young rascals would open their ears and understand these things. It is a game of patience. Nobody in human flesh should take matters into their own hands.

[Enter Oche-ilo-eze]

Oche-ilo-eze: Akaeze, I know the blame is on my head. But I assure the throne that everything is being done to expose the beasts that did this thing. We shall see the deep end of the matter.

Akaeze: I am not impressed, Oche-ilo-eze. I drew your ears early enough to the need for vigilance. A single palm fruit entrusted to your watch should not for any reason, disappear in the fire.

Oche-ilo-eze: I take the blame in so far as that vast space is under my watch. The shame is not on the white man but on the minder of the King's Square. That is me, the oche-ilo-eze. I make no excuses, but this was a coward's move by some bastards. They just exploited our human fatigue from the festival exertions.

Oyidi'a: We only thank the gods that the man wasn't killed.

Akaeze: He could have died even from mere suffocation.

Oyidi'a :   It was a very bad thing! To tie a man like that and leave him on the bare ground all night long. A white man at that!

Akaeze: Ask me what mouth Umudimkpa would have found to tell that kind of story. That a white man who visited us in peace has been killed like a festival goat!

Oyidi'a: That would have been the end of words! Ubulu which has been seeking occasion would have found it in the white man's anger.

Akaeze: We must probe this matter to the very roots.

Oche-ilo-eze: I have begun my investigations, Akaeze, and I'm already hearing some interesting stories. You must have heard what Ajofia did.

Oyidi'a: We heard that he took sand from the King's Square.

[Oche-ilo-eze grins and takes a seat]

Oche-ilo-eze: I was there. So was Orimili Obiora, both of us speaking to the Gosiora and Osilike boys. Then Ajofia arrived with his two daughters and collected the sacred sand of the King's Square. I know the power in that sand. So, I am not surprised that things of mystery are already happening.

Akaeze: I hope you are not going to tell us that it is the sand that tied the white man!

Oche-ilo-eze: It's like you have not heard, but the news is hot in the whole kingdom. Those men of yesterday who molested the girls, the sand of the King's Square has risen against them, Akaeze. The men were attacked on their way by a swarm of angry bees! Bees, Akaeze! The fools were so badly stung... their headman ran mad in the forest!

Oyidi'a: Is it for nothing that Ajofia is a dread? That man is like that. Instant revenge! No mercy at all!

Oche-ilo-eze: There cannot be mercy in the theft of cassava tubers! If a stubborn stranger would not heed a sitting advice, a common ant may teach him that certain grounds are not free seat for careless buttocks.

Akaeze: It goes to prove why I refused to consider Ajofia as a suspect in all this. He could never have involved himself in tying up the white man with common ropes. He didn't need to.

Oche-ilo-eze: The ropes thing is an outrage. I can't see how any son of the soil would be part of it. I am truly shuddering in the inside. We all know the power of the curse that rises from the King's Square.

Oyidi'a: I worry about our hot-headed youths. How informed are they about these things?

Oche-ilo-eze: The young men of Osilike were all there when I threw up the sacred sands; they heard me invoke the curse of the forefathers. Except there is any among them who takes his own foofoo through the nose, I can't see a true born committing a violation like this one. It will bring worse than death upon the offender and his entire family.

Akaeze: But the offenders were not spirits. They were some human idiots. They went to the King's Square under your watch and tied up a white man. What I want from you is their names.

[Oche-ilo-eze gets to his feet]

Oche-ilo-eze: Whatever it takes, Akaeze, I shall get you the names before sunset.

Oyidi'a: But what is this new talk about Iwobi?

Oche-ilo-eze: Hmm! I have sent someone to check out that one as well. The Iwobi we all know is paralysed from head to feet. He has not been seen outside his hut for two years now. But the white man uttered some strange things about him yesterday. He said it openly that Iwobi is tying people all over the place!

Oyidi'a: Iwobi tying people? Tying them with what? Aha, aha, are we to believe then that Iwobi tied the white man as well?

Oche-ilo-eze: I wonder who can answer that one.

Oyidi'a: I don't understand it . . . . Was he alluding to witchcraft?

Oche-ilo-eze: I don't even know what to think or believe.

Oyidi'a: Somebody tied up the white man. Whether it is Iwobi or anyone else, if the person did it by witchcraft, how can we prove guilt?

Oche-ilo-eze: It is a very difficult matter. From what I heard, it was even the white man himself who started the offensive yesterday. He told people out there that his heart will fly out like a bat to fight Iwobi. That is a clear witchcraft challenge!

Akaeze: We cannot intervene in a battle of witches. But a stranger who does not speak our language will not get tied up with physical ropes before our very eyes. We are not going to tell the whole world that we don't know the one amongst us who did this thing. You will find me the culprit, Oche-ilo-eze.

Oche-ilo-eze: Before the sun goes down, you will hear from me.

[Exit Oche-ilo-eze]

Oyidia: I still don't understand this white man, Akaeze. Why was he alone in that place? What about all those guards who wear his type of clothes?

Akaeze: Our bearded visitor does not behave like his big brother at Ubulu. You and I know that.

Oyidi'a: He is quite different. He seems to like our people . . . and I get this feeling that he really wants to be our friend.

Akaeze: Yesterday morning when he paid us a visit in this palace, he arrived with only the interpreter; not a single bodyguard, and none of those hateful bullies that follow his brother everywhere.

Oyidi'a: His fighting men were waiting at the Square. They were the ones who broke the water pots. I hear he got there and drove them away.

Akaeze: Yes, from what I learnt this morning, he was shouting at them and was very upset about the broken pots.

Oyidi'a: Permit me a little speculation. Is it possible they are the ones who . . . . ?

Akaeze: Don't even imagine it!

Oyidi'a: You think it is impossible?

Akaeze: They aren't that smart or stupid! Tie their white god? You don't know these ones. Our fellow blacks tremble when the white man farts. Some will eat his shit.

Oyidi'a: I think you are right. It couldn't have been his own men.

Akaeze: Oyidi'a, the men you are talking about, are they not the ones the bees tormented? Do you know what it is to be stung by angry bees?

Oyidi'a: I forgot that bit, Akaeze. The men would be in terrible pain. A few stings of those creatures could drive a fellow mad.

Akaeze: They must be somewhere now, fighting for dear life, not even remembering who is called master or what is called rope.

Oyidi'a: Getting treatment would take days.

Akaeze: Death could be quicker, perhaps even sweeter.

Oyidi'a: But what about that interpreter? Nobody is talking of him.

Akaeze: He too disappeared since yesterday. The white man was alone all evening. No one seems to know why.

Oyidi'a: Why would he choose to spend the night alone in the open square? Does it make any sense?

Akaeze: It is said that a man who tarries long enough in the open square will begin to see the spirits. Perhaps he was there to test his personal charms.

Oyidi'a: Perhaps those charms failed him at the critical time.

Akaeze: But it is not charms that tied him with a rope.

Oyidi'a: Akaeze, I think we need a proper talk with this white man. We must find that interpreter.

Akaeze: What if he too has gone back to Ubulu?

Oyidi'a: Did *ekwe* report and we didn't hear? He couldn't have left our borders.

Akaeze: You are right; he must still be somewhere in the villages. It won't be too hard to find out.

Oyidi'a: I hope the bees don't reach him ahead of us.

Akaeze: I hope he doesn't run mad too!

[Fade]

ACT 2, SCENE 2

Throne room at Umudimkpa palace. Akaeze holds court, Oyidi'a, Mmanko and Orimili Obiora sitting with him. Ndukwe and Ifeka are standing before them.

Ndukwe: I can swear that no member of the Gosiora Age Grade touched that man with a rope. How can we be so mundane when the power of the soil is already fighting for us?

Ifeka: Orimili Obiora, you spoke to us yesterday. It was hard, but you calmed our nerves. Osilike did not tie that white man with a common rope. The curses we hurled at him are more vicious than ropes.

Orimili Obiora: Somebody tied him with a rope.

Ndukwe: As far as we know, it is the unseen hands of our forefathers that did that one. We expect more of their intervention since the elders have told us to leave matters to the gods.

Mmanko: Our forefathers are still powerful. Nobody can defeat them.

Ndukwe: It is my personal opinion that the white man deserved those ropes. He came out there to test the power of our masquerade.

Ifeka: Even worse, he boasted that he would undress the masquerades.

Ndukwe: Now, he couldn't even untie himself. What's the difference between him and the chicken in my back yard?

[Orimili Obiora rises to his feet]

Orimili Obiora: Akaeze Right Hand of Majesty, Oyidi'a Express Image of Her Husband, Mmanko Sharp Machete that Slays in One Cut, I stand in greetings.

All three: Orimili!

Orimili Obiora: I have interviewed these leaders of Gosiora and Osilike here in your presence and you have heard their words.

Mmanko: They have anger in their voices but they are full of denials. How can we say?

Orimili Obiora: Nothing beclouds the fresh breath of innocence like the rush of utterance in the heat of passion; but that is the nature of youth. Ndukwe and Ifeka have spoken from the heart. There is a lot of heat but it seems by their words that they know how better to use their own ropes.

[A pause. Everyone is brooding. Akaeze grunts]

Akaeze: When a young man is advised to release a bit, it means his closed fist is holding more than is healthy for him. You must advise both age grades to mind their utterances.

Oyidi'a: Throwing words about like murderous objects, is that proof of manhood? Is it good manners?

Ifeka: Our apologies, High Mother.

Ndukwe: We did not intend to sound disrespectful; but the white man . . . .

Oyidi'a: Be careful with words of threat. That is wisdom. The young tortoise did not have that wisdom when he threatened a pregnant woman that he would stomp her to death in the market place. When the next day, there was a stampede in the market, the pregnant woman was stomped to death. We all know that tortoise has no stomping type of feet. He was not even in the market that day; but still, he became the main suspect in that murder case. Your threatening is just too much.

Ndukwe: We stand corrected, High Mother.

Akaeze: You may leave, young men.

Ndukwe & Ifeka: As Akaeze pleases.

[Exeunt Ndukwe & Ifeka]

Akaeze: We must look beyond the two groups. Foolishness tends to sprout where it is least expected.

[Enter Dikeogu, slaps his cowhide fan on his stool and sits]

Dikeogu: My own view of the matter is that we are overflogging it. A head pad should not be heavier than the load it is meant for.

Orimili Obiora: The matter is heavy enough, Dikeogu. Anyone who saw the white man in the condition we found him this morning would not dismiss it so lightly.

Dikeogu: I came over as soon as I was told. You all who got there before me had untied the man I saw there. That was the right thing to do and I said so, didn't I? The man has since gone about his business as if nothing happened. Why then are we breaking our own heads?

Orimili Obiora: He is our guest. Whether we approved of his visit or not, he is here with us, and I believe that every guest is good for that prayer of our fathers which you quoted yesterday. A visit should neither kill a host nor afflict his guest with the hunch-back disease.

Dikeogu: This visitor is different. He has become an uncommon affliction. What is it he wanted overnight in the King's Square? And what is he still doing there?

Mmanko: I too have many questions for that white man. Many questions!

Dikeogu: We are not the ones that tied him up. We don't even know if it is a game he is playing, what game it is and who are his playmates.

Akaeze: I hear you well, Dikeogu. I hear you very well. But it is said that a pretty face does not deserve a rage of finger nails. I don't want us to use a thing that is meant for scratching the ear to scratch out our very eye. Tell me in direct words, how do you want us to handle this matter?

Dikeogu: We should send the white man packing to the evil forest!

Mmanko: Dikeogu has spoken my mind. We said it yesterday.

Oyidi'a: Should we rush him to the evil forest when we don't know his assailants of last night? That could be dangerous.

Orimili Obiora: I think we should embrace caution, for the avoidance of blame. What has just happened is temerity in a shrine. In the forest, it would have been a full-blown rampage. Let us not put ourselves in a position to be held answerable for the white man's beard when we can't even guess his whereabouts.

Dikeogu: It appears that we are dealing with a clever rogue who knows how to get everybody's attention. Yesterday, he offered us nice presents; we rightly refused all of that because Mgbe Dike will not dance with gifts from a total stranger. Then, the man goes to the main place of the festival and camps there like an evil masquerade. Today, we find him tied up like a community ram that juveniles have prepared for sacrifice. And now, we are falling over ourselves to give him everything he wants—or rather, what we think he wants.

Orimili Obiora: It is in our own interest to put that man under day and night surveillance until he departs from our midst.

Akaeze: That is what we should do and that is what we are trying to do. Let his blood be on his own head after he moves out of our sight to the evil forest.

Oyidi'a: I've already asked Oche-ilo-eze's wives to take food and water to him. I hear he had nothing to eat all of yesterday.

Dikeogu: But how long is he going to stay in the King's Square?

Akaeze: If he told you, let us hear it.

[Awkward silence as everyone looks away]

Oyidi'a: This white man and us, we need to get word across to each other. Let him know our mind and let us know his own mind too. We have to find that interpreter.

Akaeze: The ekwe is out on him. I expect return word from the scouts.

Mmanko: I don't know if anybody heard the ekwe this morning as I did. It was hailing Ajofia. Then it asked if the interpreter woke up well. I thought that was an unusual greeting.

Dikeogu: I too thought it was a strange question. But when I heard the tale of the patriot bees, it began to make sense.

Mmanko: Those bees have made my heart very glad for Umudimkpa. It is how things should be. I am all eager to shake Ajofia's hand. Gbam!

Dikeogu: Akaeze would remind me that elders must swallow pain. But I maintain that we are overdoing it in this kingdom. We swallow too much and our children are watching; when they begin to mistake it all for a delicacy, my fears are deep.

Orimili Obiora: Have you tried talking to Gosiora and Osilike? It is now like war against us. The ones coming behind them are even more unmanageable! But as elders and nobles, we must wear the cap of maturity on a cool head always.

Dikeogu: Time is not on our side. We should do more of this thing that Ajofia has done—take even more drastic actions, prove we are warriors!

Mmanko: Dikeogu has spoken my mind!

Dikeogu: Let's do things as who we are, not sit here forever, agonizing about a stranger who gets himself tied up at the King's Square.

Akaeze : Dikeogu, you are leading the effort to move that fellow from there to the evil forest. Send him bees, scorpions, lions—anything but children of men! Let him suffer terrible things which nobody can trace to any living person's address. But remember that none of us can speak his language. You need his interpreter very badly. I was hoping that someone here may tell us where to find him for you.

Dikeogu: I did not expect this princely assignment, Akaeze; but I will do my duty to the kingdom as always.

Akaeze: That is the spirit. It is the unexpected that proves the mettle.

Oyidi'a: Once we find that interpreter, we shall resolve every aspect of this matter once and for all.

[Enter Echezo, bows before the empty throne and to Akaeze]

Echezo: Akaeze, Right Hand of Majesty, there is a word of interest. But the fellow insists on speaking to the high chiefs in person.

Akaeze: Bring him in.

[Enter Ebili, calabash slung on his shoulder]

Ebili: Worthy fathers, please do not think I am drunk. I have not set foot in this palace since night fell at high noon that terrible day many years ago . . . I want to say something very quickly, then I can leave the sad memories of this place. It's about the interpreter. The ekwe is searching for him. My heart is so troubled about that man.

Akaeze: Do you have any information where he is?

Ebili: I worry more who he is and where he came from. I feel I know him and I don't seem to know him. It worried me all night.

Dikeogu: What manner of drunken talk have you brought here? You feel you know him and you don't seem to know him.

Ebili: That man knows your son. I heard the names Apiti and Ebili in his mouth. He was talking to the white man.

Mmanko: Since when did you start hearing white man's language? Can you see what too much palm wine is doing to your head?

Ebili: Please don't think I am drunk . . .

Akaeze: What we think of you should not matter. The ekwe is clear on what we need from you. If you get more useful information on the man, come back to me.

Ebili: See, the man called Apiti and Ebili with his mouth. How did he know the names? I heard him very well. But you think I'm drunk . . .

[Fade]

ACT 2, SCENE 3

Throne Room at Umudimkpa palace. Oche-ilo-eze is standing before the high chiefs. It is about noon.

Oche-ilo-eze: Akaeze, the kolanut of valour should be kept ready. What Ajofia has done will fill your ears. It is again like the time of old!

Akaeze: Certain bad feet walked the Square last night. I asked you for names, Oche-ilo-eze. Have you got them now?

Oche-ilo-eze: It is as the saying goes, Akaeze: Every find is there in the bag of the medicine man. Ajofia will soon be here, and his own mouth will speak for him because what he told me is too big for another mouth to tell.

Mmanko: Now you are causing my ear to itch.

Oche-ilo-eze: You will hear more than you can hold, I tell you!

Dikeogu: Nobody is allowed to dribble us here. If you have any report for us, pour it out or leave.

Oche-ilo-eze: Ajofia insists that he wants to tell you by himself. A hunter's tale is sweetest in his own mouth.

Orimili Obiora: Here he comes whose name is fresh in mouths and ears!

[Enter Ajofia, rear first]

Oche-ilo-eze: Ajofia himself!

Mmanko: Burden of Horrors!

Oche-ilo-eze: Jungle of Dread Steps and Mystic Dances!

Mmanko: Evil Fog that Screens the Moon from View!

Dikeogu: Ajofia, Igiligi Ogu! Ominous Mist of Combat!

[Ajofia, slow and deliberate, leans his staff in the rack, removes the palm frond bit from between his jaws, and surveys the session. Oche-ilo-eze takes a stool in the far corner]

Ajofia *[mid-way to his stool]*:   Ajofia pays his respects to the throne. Akaeze, Oyidi'a, brother high chiefs, you are worthy of your high stools.

Akaeze: Ajofia, The One-Man That Is Saluted As A Multitude!

Ajofia: Akaeze!

Akaeze: News of your exploits has filled our ears with anxiety.

Ajofia: I don't know what you heard. My hands are innocent.

Dikeogu: Is Innocent the new name of angry bees? Admirable!

Mmanko *[springing to his feet]*:   Receive my hand!

[Mmanko gives him that elaborate handshake of titled men—three backhanded steals preceding the clasp. Dikeogu does same, a little less spiritedly, from his seat.]

Orimili Obiora: A man whose name is mentioned in every discussion must be doing something special!

Ajofia: What did I do but swat a few houseflies? Why should that be news?

[Ajofia slaps his stool with his large cowhide fan; sits down.]

Dikeogu: It is like the patriot bees of old are back in business; they make news by stinging public fools!

Akaeze: Next on standby must be tsetse flies!

Mmanko: Even scorpions!

Ajofia: Akaeze, what choice is left for *onye achonam*, a lone
            wayfarer who has no wish to offend or be offended? When
            you withdraw to your own quiet corner for a private nap,
            the idiots of this age tell themselves that you are finished.
            They begin to gloat and do foolish, annoying things. So, you
            shake your body a little. Just to show people that you are
            still there. A live fire may diminish itself but it can never be
            enfolded in anybody's loin cloth.

Mmanko: Gbam! Please have it again!

            [Mmanko repeats the handshake with Ajofia]

Oyidi'a: What about my daughters whose pots were broken? I hope
            they have wiped their tears?

Ajofia: Nobody will ever trouble them again. I will tell you things,
            Oyidi'a.

Oyidi'a: I will be glad to hear.

Mmanko: It feels great again to be Umudimkpa! Yesterday was shame
            worse than death. All of us, the men folk in this land, are we
            eunuchs?

Ajofia: I decided to do something about the provocation because
            it was getting out of hand. If early trespassers are not
            challenged, their footprints turn a man's compound into a
            public thoroughfare.

Dikeogu: It was clear even to mere infants that something had to
            happen. We had become spectators to our day-by-day
            extinction. This thing that Ajofia did has to be done again
            and again.

Mmanko: Gbam!

Akaeze: Ajofia will tell us what was done. It is when we hear the tune of the bullhorn that we shall know the dance step.

[Ajofia rises to his feet]

Ajofia: Akaeze, I salute the throne and I salute you.

Akaeze: Umudimkpa salutes Ajofia, for the wisdom in his mouth.

Ajofia: Akaeze, the he-lizard must prove himself a he-lizard; otherwise, little children would mistake him in the rain for another wet stick and gather him as off-season firewood.

Mmanko: That is true!

Ajofia: What Ajofia did is not a matter of long, long talk. But the result is now smiling back at us. There are four agents of the white man who will never again mistake us for wet sticks. I have them like this in my left hand now. Umudimkpa, speak as men and tell me what you want. Shall they be broken, burnt, beheaded or buried alive?

Mmanko *[up on his feet]*: That is how it used to be. *[Repeats his handshake with Ajofia]*

Akaeze: Who are these four, Ajofia? The fighting men who broke the water pots?

Ajofia: Three of those ones. The fourth, their headman has disappeared. I hear he ran mad somewhere in the forest. The rest came begging for life and sanity. Umudimkpa, which one should I deny them?

Akaeze: This is beyond words! And it is, speaking for all Umudimkpa, a feat worthy of *oji nwadike,* the kola of valour. But who is the fourth captive?

Ajofia: That one will surprise you all. But I can spare you the guess work. I hear you are searching for him already.

Oyidi'a: Not the interpreter?

Ajofia: The white man's abusive mouthpiece! That's the one. He personally brought the three to my residence, humbled and pleading.

Akaeze: You have the interpreter!

Ajofia: He is there with the three. They all spent the night in my *obi*, promising this and that.

Akaeze: This one is beyond words!

Orimili: It has eaten up my mouth. Ajofia, *Akilika!* Tough and Resolute Thatch!

Dikeogu: But do you trust that interpreter?

Akaeze: How can I trust a snake? It is my powerful charms I trusted and they caught him for us.

Dikeogu: There is something about that man, something I can't figure out which makes me very uncomfortable. That drunk they call Ebili was saying something like that but you know my views about that bunch . . .Anyway, you are right to regard this one as a snake.

Ajofia: Ajofia is nobody's fool. Before I swallow, I peck to pieces like mother hen. I put the fellow to a test last night and you all saw the result this morning!

Akaeze: What result, what test?

Ajofia *[with a dry laugh]*:   When they begged and begged last night, I was so disgusted I just wanted to see them out of my compound. I said to them 'Your white master, does he know that hot water is fatal to tortoise? Go and teach him sense. Take a rope and go tie him up, then come back and we can talk.' They went straight and did it!

Akaeze: Ajo-ofia!

Oyidi'a: What a blaze!

Akaeze: So you are the one who put us in a leaky skiff?

Ajofia: Blame the laity. They are a confused mob that takes every word literally. I never expected this, even from brainless cocoyams!

Mmanko: You forget your own powers. When you put those spices in your mouth, who can disobey your order?

Oche-ilo-eze [rising to his feet]: Oche-ilo-eze greets the palace. My own part is done. I am relieved—vindicated too. I knew from the beginning that no son of the soil would dare violate the sanctity of the King's Square. We all know the power of that soil. The curse shall be on the head of those strangers. I shall go and pour the normal libation.

Ajofia: Umudimkpa, those four men are still in my house. I am still asking. Tell me what you want.

Akaeze: You have done well to ask, Ajofia. There are things that must be said to the white man. We need that interpreter to take our message to him. How quickly can you bring him here?

Ajofia: I plead on his behalf for our understanding. He and his men want to lie very low for a few days. He will come by night to see you immediately after the festival.

Akaeze: It makes sense, I think. Is there a different view?

Dikeogu: Not at all, not at all.

Akaeze: As for the three fighting men, you will use your wisdom, but avoid the white man's trouble. A visit should not bring harm to host or guest; besides, the captive we show mercy today may save a life tomorrow.

           [Enter Echezo, waving an envelope. He bows]

Echezo: Akaeze, Odikpo has brought this from his father in the prison. He said one of the white man's fighting men gave it to him this morning.

Akaeze *[suspiciously and reluctant to touch the envelope]:* What is this one?

Echezo: It is white man's way of sending an important message. Odikpo said his father paid someone to do it for him because there is a very important message which must get to Akaeze. It is inside it.

[With evident curiosity and ginger hands, Akaeze and Echezo fumble with it and finally succeed in opening it. They pull out and examine the letter]

Akaeze: It is white man's paper with white man's written things. But who can read what is written here for us?

Oche-ilo-eze: None of our people has acquired the white man's art. We will have to send to Ubulu for help.

Ajofia: That would not be necessary, Akaeze. The interpreter is there in my house. He will decode it for us.

Akaeze *[much relieved]:* That is perfect. Some payback from him for all your hospitality. *[Hands the letter to Ajofia who puts it in his goatskin bag]*

Oyidi'a: Akaeze, is it in order now to present *oji nwa dike*, the kola of valour?

Akaeze: It cannot wait, Oyidi'a. We shall eat that kola with the pride of the ancient warriors. Please include alligator pepper. It never goes on a shameful trip.

Oche-ilo-eze *[regaining his seat]*: In that case, I should tarry awhile. I am not the horn of a goat that always misses out on a feast.

[Exit Oyidi'a]

Mmanko: I am the happiest man in the country now. My anger yesterday was enough to kill a whole market. Whose common dog entered Umudimkpa and broke our daughters' water pots? What gave them the boldness?

Dikeogu: The same kind of thing that prompted Monkey to challenge Baboon to a wrestling contest. It is a disease that is worse than madness. Very common in this age!

Akaeze: Orimili Obiora, I thought you would say something to that. It is your age that would wrestle baboon or gorilla for just about anything.

Orimili Obiora: My humble view accepts that life is a struggle. Akaeze, there are fights a man cannot avoid if he must give a meaning to his life. My father taught me that *oji ofo ga ana*. A mandate that is rooted in equity shall always prevail.

Ajofia: Your father, the great Orimili was right on that point. A stranger who refuses a fellow man the right to sit down in his own home is asking for an ugly fight.

Dikeogu: It is worse if I neither invited the meddling stranger nor complained to him that sitting is costing me a testicle.

Ajofia: But that is the white man and his agents! They have become an evil boil on the testicle of the small *nza*. Treating it is castration, ignoring it a painful death. Ajofia has played his own part in the matter. Let us make up our minds what future we all want.

Mmanko: We must fight as men. Yes! It feels good again to be Umudimkpa!

[*Re-enter Oyidi'a, a maid before her bearing a wooden platter of kola nuts and alligator pepper*]

Oyidi'a: Fathers of the kingdom, Igwe's kola is here.

Akaeze: If it is kola of valour, hand it over to Orimili Obiora to do the tradition. He is the youngest titled man here.

[*Orimili Obiora rises and takes the platter. The maid exits*]

Orimili Obiora: I hold this kola on behalf of my superiors as I only received it as a messenger. The kindling fire that an elder has packaged for a child will not burn his hand. I await your telling nod, Akaeze.

Akaeze: Proceed, Orimili. There is no fear.

Orimili Obiora: I will not dare break kola in the presence of my worthy seniors.

Akaeze: You are well brought up, Orimili Obiora.

Dikeogu: It is good to see that the eagle feather that so fits his cap has not gone into his head as we see in the youth of these times.

Oyidi'a: It's hardly the fault of the youths. How much are they being taught these days?

Akaeze: You are right Oyidi'a. We must continually rehearse these things to drill them down. It is said that saying nothing is a failing of elders, hearing nothing the fault of the youths.

Dikeogu: As parents and grandparents, aren't we always talking and talking? It's like shouting to the stone deaf, a waste of time!

Akaeze: There is never an easy way out. So long as chewables remain in the cheeks, the jaws cannot rest in their grinding work. Tell me, Mmanko, what are the rules of *oji nwadike*, the kola of valour?

Mmanko: Is it not Akaeze that breaks it?

Akaeze [*chuckling, shakes his head*]: Let me just answer the question myself and spare everybody here any further embarrassment. *Oji nwadike* is presented by the king's household to the Igwe-in-council. It is broken by the eldest male in attendance after each of the seven high chiefs (present or not) has reserved his take-away entitlement of one whole nut.

Dikeogu: So who should break this one? Is it Oche-ilo-eze?

Akaeze: Unless anyone here is older. I believe I'm the nearest to him but still, I can't overtake him, can I?

Ajofia: Akaeze is right. *Oji nwadike* respects age above title. It goes round twice so we endorse it first; then next, we take our whole portions and reserve for each fellow high chief who isn't here. Then Oche-ilo-eze being the oldest male present will break it for general communion.

Oche-ilo-eze: I may choose not to break the kola myself. A senior reserves a right to delegate or appoint a younger man to do it for him, after a few words of blessing.

Dikeogu: The trouble with these things is memory. People do it the way they remember.

Orimili Obiora: Or the way they choose to remember . . . selfish motives!

Oche-ilo-eze: That is where the white man is different from us. Everything in his life is written in a book. That is his power over us today.

Oyidi'a: He has promised to teach our children that magic. But who is ready to send his own child?

Akaeze: That is a question each of us must answer for himself.

Dikeogu: You sound like you would even give it a thought?

Akaeze: Who knows if I shouldn't? Let us break our kola. You may proceed, Orimili Obiora.

[Orimili Obiora presents the kola to the empty throne, then passes it round to the chiefs beginning with Akaeze. All lay a right hand of endorsement, then the circulation is repeated, Akaeze selecting two whole nuts which he hands to Oyidi'a for the king before picking one for himself. The others take theirs and the platter is passed to Oche-ilo-eze in his corner.]

Oche-ilo-eze: Igwe! Akaeze! Oyidi'a! Dikeogu! Mmanko! Orimili! Ajofia! Great fathers of the land, it is your respect for the mandate of age that has put this kola in my hands. But you know that the kola of valour does not relish lengthy words. So I place my hand on this kola to put the blessing of age in it. Permit me then to refer it to a younger man who should have as much stake to the future as we have enjoyed to the present day. Let him lead this celebration by breaking the kola for us. Orimili Obiora, Umudimkpa is with you on this!

[He hands the platter back to Orimili Obiora who takes it to his seat]

Orimili Obiora: The mystique of the lion is his first line of sure defence.
Umudimkpa is like a lion, her mystique and defence being sons and daughters whose exploits strike fear in the hearts of her enemies. I break the kola you have asked me to break. *[Breaks a few nuts]* It is a testimony that someone in this land has done something that the throne and the fathers should note.

Akaeze: If such a valiant is alive, should he not be present here? And if present, should he not be called by name?

Orimili Obiora: My voice will not fail me, Akaeze. But a great name is sweetest in the mouth of melody.

Akaeze: Let us hear it.

[Orimili Obiora intones and leads the chorus. All rise, singing. Ajofia as honoree remains seated, head bowed]:

Orimili Obiora/all *[alternating]*:

    Ajofia, do-o, do-odo
    Ajofia, do-o, do-odo
    Ajofia do-o, do-odo
    Ajofia do-o, do-odo
    Oke mmanwu igbanite?
    Ajofia do-o, do-odo
    Nnukwu mmanwu igbalute?
    Ajofia do-o, do-odo

    "Ajofia, we implore you
    Ajofia, we implore you
    Great Mask are you risen?
    Great Mask are you here?
    Ajofia, we implore you"

Obiora: Onye g'etu ugo ga ete awa mmee n'isi o!
           (Whosoever will wear a plume must anoint his head with
           the blood of sprinkling!)

           Chorus *[all pointing at Ajofia]*:
           Ayeeeh, dike n'ukpo
           Ayeeeh, dike n'ukpo
           Ayeeeh, Ajofia n'ukpo
           Ugo ejugo kwa g'isi o
           Ayeeeh Ajofia n'ukpo loooh!

           Yeah, valiant be enthroned
           Yeah, valiant be enthroned
           Yeah, Ajofia be enthroned
           Your head full of eagle plumes
           Ooh! Yeah, Ajofia is enthroned

*[The platter is passed to Akaeze who picks up the alligator pepper, holds it
behind his back and cuts it open with his fingers]*

Akaeze: Kill the valiant, kill the valiant; on battle day, we seek the
           valiant. Ajofia the throne asks you to come forward for *oji
           nwadike.*

           *[Ajofia bows before the throne then stooping before Akaeze,
           takes one unbroken kola and raises it up]*

Ajofia: This is a great honour.

Akaeze: It is an endorsement of what you have done and a mandate
           to do a new exploit.

Dikeogu: It's a double mandate as this is Mgbe Dike.

Ajofia: Umudimkpa kwenu!

All: Yaa!

Ajofia: Chakenu!

All: Yaa!

Ajofia: Kwezuenu!

All: Yaa!

[Ajofia takes his seat. The platter is passed round by Orimili starting from Oche-ilo-eze . . . The refrain, Ajofia do-do-doh is floating . . . .]

[Fade]

ACT 2, SCENE 4

Throne Room at Umudimkpa Palace. Ajofia is standing beside the staff rack with Dikeogu and Mmanko. They converse in lowered tones, the mood conspiratorial.

Ajofia: It is the hand of the gods.

Dikeogu: *Oji nwa dike* for a high chief at Mgbe Dike is a once-in-a-lifetime feat! It is power to take initiatives in defence of throne and country within the few days of the festival.

Mmanko: We must seize the opportunity. Dikeogu, what of you?

Dikeogu *[pensively]:*   This is good music to my ears. Didn't you hear Akaeze? He challenged me to move the white man out of the Square without human hands. This is for me! That stranger must leave that ground tomorrow or next.

Ajofia: If we can do the right sacrifice, it is easy.

Mmanko: I have said many times, let us ask the ancient questions!

Dikeogu: My whole life is upside down. My long dead wife has started coming again. All the sacrifices I make with goats and chickens are as nothing. What will it take to question the ancients the right way?

Ajofia: Seven slave heads.

Dikeogu: I can provide that readily.

Ajofia: If we can add one head of a free-born, it is perfect.

Mmanko: Why not? We can get one from a neighbouring clan.

Ajofia: It has to be a virgin.

Mmanko: In the worst case, a daughter goes.

Dikeogu: The white man has eyes everywhere. Our own brothers spy
           for him. That is what worries me.

Ajofia: But the interpreter is giving us full assurance. He will get the
           white man out of our path or make him look the other way.
           This is our best moment. We have a useful ally in the white
           man's camp.

Dikeogu: Something still worries me about that fellow. I don't know
           why, but he wakes up long-sleeping angers in me; like I
           should put him in the mortar and pound him to a pulp.

Ajofia: I was feeling the same way until he and I talked last night.

Mmanko: I hate all the blacks who work for the white man. I curse
           them every day.

Ajofia: The interpreter is very different, but I did not know. Forget
           that face he puts out to the world. He confided last night that
           it is a borrowed face, a mask he called it. That man is full of
           native wit and cunning.

Mmanko: I feel in my body that he can help us. The gods know we
           have suffered enough shame. They brought him our way, to
           do something for us.

Ajofia: When you sit down and talk with him, you too will see that
           he is even begging to help us.

Mmanko: My body tells me that he will help. I feel it deep inside my body.

Ajofia: You know what he told me? Every kingdom has its own
           blood secret; so if blood is dismay, kingdom is deceit! That's
           what he said with his own mouth, word for word.

Dikeogu: That is a direct quote from the secret codes. It means he understands.

Ajofia: He has a full mastery. He knows the inside-out of things in this kingdom. I was surprised at the names of people he has in his head.

Dikeogu: How would he know so much and we don't know him?

Ajofia: His late mother was from these parts.

Dikeogu: What family is that?

Ajofia: He wants to be very sure before he names names. She had died giving birth to him in a strange land. He still carries the grief even though he tries to make light matter of it with clever jokes.

Dikeogu: My first wife died in childbirth. I can never forget the pain. No sane person jokes with that kind of trouble.

Ajofia: But what I've observed in my years is that most victims of tragic fate tend to mock their own grief. I think it is for sanity.

Dikeogu: It is an evil child that kills his own mother at his birth. That I know.

Ajofia: Our man relates himself to the proverbial tortoise—the one whose first daughter shut her ears and eloped for marriage; Death shut its own ears and killed the poor lady, so tortoise shut his own ears and travelled for her body. Here is a man desperate to locate his mother's family. I see him as a powerful amulet which the gods have delivered into our hands against the white man.

Mmanko: What is that name they call him?

Ajofia: Abadinegwu. Something like that . . . It is the name the white man gave him

94

Mmanko: It sounds like Abanidiegwu, The Night is Terror.

Ajofia: We better work on him to turn that terror on the white man.

Mmanko: Ise-e!

[Dikeogu has a faraway look in his eyes. A haze has appeared in the corner and there is a glimpse of a woman in white wrapper and breast-piece standing there, broom in hand. Dikeogu wavers but she drifts away]

Dikeogu: It is getting worse by the day, this torture. That was Mgbafor again . . . She comes so often these days. I see her so clearly.

Ajofia: Did you see her now?

Dikeogu: As clear as daylight. I feel her urgency: she is anxious to tell me something!

Ajofia: We must be quick to do this thing. The blood of goats and chickens can no longer hold back the spirits.

Dikeogu: I am in full agreement, Ajofia. What of you, Mmanko?

[Dikeogu holds out the open palm of his left hand. The others place theirs on top and all three cover them with their right hands.]

Mmanko: It shall be as agreed.

Ajofia: So shall it be.

Dikeogu: How quickly can we meet with him?

Ajofia: Tonight in my obi.

[Lights dim. Fade.]

95

ACT 2, SCENE 5

Ajofia's obi, the patriarch's observatory and private meeting place in the forecourt of his vast family buildings. All is dark and quiet in the late night. A small taper burns in a clay pot in a corner, casting weird shadows on the mud walls. Ajofia is closeted in a meeting with Dikeogu, Mmanko and Abednego—all sitting on the mud form against the side wall closest to his carved chair. They appear to blend in the half-light with the grim statues and effigies of idols which are peering from their various bases on rack and floor.

Ajofia: Dikeogu . . . Mmanko . . ., it is said that once a quorum is formed for the eating of vulture meat, the smoked basket must come down. You have heard with your own ears what the bullhorn is speaking.

Dikeogu: Indeed, deep matters are being revealed. But I suggest we first resolve the written message that Akaeze gave you. I hear it is called letter.

Mmanko: That is good. Let him decode it for us, then we can talk better.

[Ajofia fetches the letter from his goatskin bag and Abednego studiously reads it in halting English]

Abednego *[voice over]*:

Dear Chief,

> I am very fearfully to tell you. Dangerful man, Apiti has not dead. He is very very very alife. I see he with eye. He has new name of Abadinego. He plan bad. Bad worser than befour. You know he how he wicked and very dangerful. He has not change. Be very carefully evrybodies. Apiti has not dead.

> Yours brother
> Chime

96

[Abednego grunts, hisses and shakes his head sadly]

Dikeogu: What is it saying?

Abednego: Before I speak at all, I want to know who else has read this letter . . . I ask this important question because I don't want anybody to confuse you as they do at Ubulu.

Ajofia: No one else can read the white man's written things in the whole land. That is why we brought it to you.

Abednego: You did well to bring it to me. I have read it to myself. Now, I will interpret it for you. It is from one Chime. What kind of man is he? He sounds happy that someone is dead.

Mmanko: Who has died?

Abednego: A person called Apiti. It says here—see—'Apiti has dead'. Chime is very happy to confirm to you that Apiti is dead.

Mmanko: Chime is not the only person who is happy about that. Apiti wanted to kill all of us. Everyone is happy that he is dead.

Dikeogu: But that's no news to us. His death was reported many years back and all Umudimkpa heard it. Is that the only thing there?

Abednego: No, my own name is even mentioned. It's here—Abednego. He says (let me read it out for you. Rather, I interpret as I read) "Umudimkpa is very lucky to have one man called Abednego. He is son of our daughter. He is a very good man. Important personality. After white man, it is Abednego. All the chiefs, please listen to follow him very well so that Umudimkpa will become greatest than before. Thank you all.'

Ajofia: This is the very hand of the gods!

Mmanko: It is the gods that brought our daughter's son back to us at this time. Shake my hand, son of the native soil.

[Abednego kneels before Mmanko]

Abednego: Who am I to shake hands with my great uncles? Permit me to just kneel at your feet and your prayers will make me great.

Mmanko: Rise up, worthy son. You are already great and you will become even greater. Who can say no when Umudimkpa is saying yes to you? Whoever fights against you, this land will hunt him down and kill him for us.

Abednego: Ise-e! Thank you, great fathers. Thank you.

Mmanko: We are the one to thank you. What you have just told us, if you do it as you say, this land can never thank you enough.

Abednego: Even at the greatest risk to my life, I will do anything for my mother's people.

Dikeogu: I am still not sure what he wants from us.

Mmanko: He said that . . .

Dikeogu: Let him speak for himself.

Abednego *[retakes his seat somberly]*: It is the big white man at Ubulu that gave me the name Abednego. He is the chief of the white people, a man of great power. I started working for him only a few months ago; but now he regards me above all his other natives. He sees it and says it that I am fearless. That is why he calls me Abednego, a man who can pass through fire for something good.

Mmanko: Umudimkpa are born fearless. Our daughter's offspring cannot be different.

Abednego: What I need from my mother's people is their complete trust. Only their trust. I want to do something that no one else can dare, for the good people of this land.

Mmanko: You will do it, great son. We shall go all the way with you.

Abednego: No sacrifice is too much for the womb that birthed me, a mother who labored unto death to give me life. I have a good position with the big white man. I just want to use it for you. But I can't do much if I don't have your complete trust.

Dikeogu: Trust is not a plaything. It is the price of a warrior's life and the prize from his many battles. A stranger who demands to be trusted is like an untested trap. You may not know the catch until too late.

Abednego: But I am not a stranger. I am your son.

[A haze appears in the corner and Mgbafor materializes, broom in hand. Dikeogu gets up, moves with uncertain steps towards her. She fades]

Dikeogu *[hoarsely]*: She was here just now.

Ajofia: Your dead wife, Mgbafor?

Dikeogu: Yes.

Ajofia: That is serious, very serious. If she can walk into this place as well, then there is fire in the rafters. We cannot afford to waste a moment more.

Mmanko: Let us stop the talk. We have only two days more before Mgbe Dike ends. After the two days, this opportunity is over.

Ajofia: Are we ready to proceed, Dikeogu?

Dikeogu: I still don't understand why I am feeling like this. My head is pounding. I hear voices shouting untested trap, untested trap.

Ajofia: If you want to test our son on the codes, is there a trap in that?

Abednego: Traps do not prevent a test of courage.

Dikeogu *[goes to a corner and faces the side wall]*:
So what separates the stranger from family?

Abednego *[walks over, stands back-to-back with Dikeogu]*:
Neither sleep nor the colour of blood.

Dikeogu: What about the lamentations of deep night?

Abednego: It was mother owl, calling her daughter's face a horror mask.

Dikeogu: The owl has one complaint only: she cannot bear the ugliness of her daughter's face.

Abednego: It may sound rude to speak of resemblance.

Dikeogu: What say have palm fruits as exhibits?

Abednego: When a woman is looking for real trouble from her husband, she demands for palm oil to eat palm nuts.

Dikeogu: What is the winning argument in the forest of elephants?

Abednego: The silence of trees, standing or fallen.

Dikeogu: Was there no dispute outside the barn?

Abednego: Only the confessions of a he-goat that his affair with his own mother is wrong and distasteful but a matter of ca-ca-ca-can't help!

Dikeogu: What was the madman's dilemma in the heat of the market?

Abednego: The tumult was making him dizzy with sleep but he dared not shut his eyes because of fear that he might wake up and not find his head.

Dikeogu: What has the bat declared as eye witness?

Abednego: Lady Bat accepts that her own looks would never win her a beauty pageant; and that is why she has elected night travels. If she must fly by day, it must be with eyes shut.

Dikeogu: Was the crab not aware of these facts?

Abednego: The crab is the greatest swimmer of the mighty waves, a veteran of glorious exploits and legendary acrobatics in the deep waters. But fate, the eternal mocker of fame, has one special reception for him—the final swim in an old woman's soup pot!

Dikeogu [nodding, impressed, returning]: He sounds even more direct our son than our daughter's born.

Ajofia: It is as I told you. His mastery of the codes is faultless.

Mmanko [gives Abednego the chieftaincy handshake]: Receive my hand, son of our great daughter. You deserve the honour.

Dikeogu: But I still want to hear more about his work for the white man.

Abednego: The white man and I are very close. I'm talking of D.O. the big man at Ubulu. Not this preaching one that dispenses words and words, thinking that long talk can change a people's way of life.

Mmanko: But all the whites are tight brothers. They are doing everything to confuse us with words so they can take over our land. They like it when we quarrel but they themselves gum together and nothing divides them.

Abednego: They are not as united as our people think, these white folks. They have their own dog fights. We who are in there with them, our eyes see many, many things.

Mmanko: It is good to hear this. But why do they have to quarrel with themselves?

Abednego: They quarrel like children—over anything and everything, but they are very good at pretending. You see this preaching one? He never thinks of safety for himself. He can go anywhere, anytime. That's why his brother, the D.O. believes he is mad; he told me in secret to watch him very closely.

Dikeogu: So, why did you leave him alone at the King's Square?

Abednego: His utterances! I don't know if you heard. He told the people that he would stand and they would miss. That's not all. He said he would undress the masquerades! When a man spews that kind of poison, he wants to die alone.

[Hisses of disgust and anger, all seeing with Abednego]

Ajofia: Is it true he also accused Iwobi of witchcraft?

Abednego: It was a complete exposure of that man called Iwobi. He's been lying on sick bed but using his secret powers to tie up many people.

Dikeogu: Nothing has been proved of that allegation. If the white man had any repect for elders, he would have reported his suspicions to us; not go there and shout to the whole world that someone is a witch. He has put Iwobi in an awful condition and the fellow could be lynched.

Ajofia: Everything is pointing to the battle front. The gods offer us a last chance to redeem the land and there is no time to lose.

Mmanko: Seven slave heads and one head of a free-born virgin girl.

Dikeogu: I shall provide all seven slaves.

Ajofia: Do five. I'll do two.

Mmanko: Leave the virgin girl to me.

Ajofia: The victims must be brought live before the Agbala shrine.

Mmanko: What night shall it be—tomorrow or next?

Dikeogu & Ajofia *[in unison]*:   Tomorrow!

[Dikeogu holds out the open palm of his left hand. His two colleagues place theirs on top and all three cover the pile with their right hands in a solemn gesture of solidarity. Abednego applauds, clapping his hands. Lights dim. Blackout.]

ACT 3, SCENE 1

Throne room at Umudimkpa palace. Oyidi'a and a girl of twelve, clad like her in white knee-length wrapper tied above the breasts, are slowly walking around the palace. Oyidi'a mutters prayers and sprinkles white chalk powder with helpings from an earthen bowl on the girl's head.

Oyidi'a *[praying]*:   What we do not know shall not know us
          What we forbid shall not find us
          As a new day opens her door, so we open our mouths
          What we eat shall come fresh
          Whatever would eat us, flee and perish far from us.

Maid: Ise-e!

Oyidi'a: Throne and kingdom shall dwell in peace
          As no fist can pluck down the sky above
          And no thirst can empty the great river
          And no fist can shove this earth out of place
          So shall each market day bring peace and speak joy.

Maid: Ise-e!

Oyidi'a: Strangers have desecrated the groves
          Alien masks parade themselves unchecked
          But beasts of the land cannot fly in the air
          And fishes of the lake can never walk on land
          So no forbidden thing shall approach this throne.

Maid: Ise-e!

[Enter Akaeze. He waits by the door, letting Oyidi'a round off her ministrations]

Oyidi'a: There is one for whom the kingdom waits
          Our yearning hearts of days and years we hold
          The sky is ageless, her patience endless

As the count of days will never cease in the sky
So shall our yearning stretch till the king is come.

Maid: Ise-e!

Oyidi'a: Noble seed, wherever you are, I call you forth
            From rock or iron clam, I prise you forth
            From storms and snares, I call you forth
            Evil shall never overtake your ordained response
            The sky that reserves your place shall preserve your day.

Maid: Ise-e!

[Oyidi'a waves the girl away, rubs her hands together and holds them awhile to her face, then greets Akaeze]

Oyidi'a: Akaeze, your early feet brighten the palace.

Akaeze: It was a great relief to meet your morning prayer. I had to
            come this early, Oyidi'a. I had a terrible dream.

            [Akaeze sits; Oyidi'a follows, much worried]

Oyidi'a: Ah! I had a very bad one too. An evil masquerade broke into
            this palace and . . .

Akaeze: And what?

Oyidi'a: Sat on the throne.

Akaeze: Deadliest of all the forbidden things! The gods will stand
            with us. But my own dream was no better . . .A dreadful
            wind hit this palace and blew off the whole roof.

Oyidi'a: It is an emergency then. Either something has gone very
            wrong or it is about to kick us in the face.

Akaeze: Oyidi'a, I fear the worst. The utterances of the white preacher have dug an evil pit. Some unknown men stormed Iwobi's house last night and abducted his little daughter.

Oyidi'a: Ewo! Which one of them?

Akaeze: The eleven- or twelve-year old called Uzoma, his daughter by Nnenna, his third wife.

Oyidi'a: Ewo! Ewo! This is unbearable. Where can we find words to console poor Nnenna?

Akaeze: It is not Nnenna only. All of us are victims. But first thing, Oyidi'a, we must get that white man out of the Square before he utters more trouble.

Oyidi'a: You've already put Dikeogu in charge of that task. We agreed yesterday.

Akaeze: With what has just happened, I must get involved as well. It is an emergency.

Oyidi'a: But what manner of wickedness is this? Who wants to mock a sick man like Iwobi in this fashion? Such a mean blow at the lowest point of a man's life!

Akaeze: It is high malice and base cowardice—as if to show the dying man that he is nothing. A vile and wicked taunt, like "Are you a man? Get up and protect your family if you are a man!"

Oyidi'a: It is really very unfortunate in the very thick of Mgbe Dike.

Akaeze: It is very painful. Very, very painful.

Oyidi'a: But what is Mmanko doing about the violation of his domain? Iwobi is his neighbour.

Akaeze: Mmanko has been quick as always. He sent me a firm
           assurance that his men are trailing the abductors. But I am
           not leaving it to him alone. This is a challenge to the whole
           kingdom. That girl must be found—and I mean, found
           alive!

Oyidi'a: The gods will help us.

Akaeze: Oyidi'a, it may be true that the grunt of an old leopard can
           never match the growl of his youth times. But when the fires
           of battle days are rekindled in old bones, the tired steps of
           aged folks regain the bounce and spring of a killing hunt. I
           am back on the hunting trail, Oyidia, and I will personally
           lead the charge. If a single case of abduction is allowed to
           succeed in our land, the whole kingdom is nothing but a
           captive goat.

[Enter Orimili Obiora]

Orimili Obiora: Oyidi'a, Akaeze, I bend double in due greetings.

Akaeze: Orimili Obiora, you are in good time.

Oyidi'a: Step up, *Omekannia*, Great son who behaves just like his
           father!

Orimili Obiora: Mother of all, I doubt if my father would be proud of
           me this awkward morning. I am trembling like a day-old
           chick.

Akaeze: Only a lifeless stone sits unmoved by such bad news. I've
           sent for everyone. We must meet quickly and take very
           urgent decisions.

Orimili Obiora: Akaeze, that girl, Uzoma is the closest friend and
           playmate of my daughter, Adaobi. She was in my house
           yesterday till late evening. Adaobi even walked her part of
           the way back. The bad story of this morning, I am lost for

words. I feel like it is my own Adaobi that those evil hawks have carried away!

Akaeze: My immediate thought is—let Ajofia produce that interpreter so we can send word to the white preacher. Let him know what his strange remark about Iwobi has caused. That is, if he doesn't know already.

Orimili Obiora: We must get him to leave that square as discussed.

Akaeze: He has become an undeniable distraction, the entry point of foul water that pollutes the sweet pumpkin.

Orimili Obiora: From what Nnenna, the girl's mother is saying, the men who did this are not outsiders. She said she heard them very well in the dark; and it was our very dialect they spoke.

Oyidi'a: What is their motive or grouse? If Iwobi bewitched someone, who is the victim; what is the proof?

Orimili Obiora: The white preacher must explain the basis of his allegations. They are grievous and wild and unacceptable. The Iwobi I have known and admired from childhood is a very decent man. He doesn't deserve this at all.

Akaeze: Custom spells out very clearly the rules to follow in dealing with witches. It is not like this at all. No one has brought a complaint against Iwobi. And no one should call him a witch just because a total stranger made an allegation that no one understands.

Orimili Obiora: It is really unfortunate that anyone could harbor such a depth of ill will for a man like Iwobi. It's like they found cover in the white man's words for a long-nurtured evil.

Akaeze: Whoever did it has got us to contend with. We will gather all clues. Before noon, we must be up to something definite.

Orimili Obiora: But Mgbe Dike enters the third day of celebrations today. The abductors may find cover in the heat of activities.

Akaeze: I have ordered the royal hunters to search every inch of every compound, starting with my own. There will be no exception for anybody. Let me see where they can hide her in this kingdom.

Orimili Obiora: What if they lie low and move by night?

Akaeze: It will be even harder for them. We are putting *Ajukwu* in action every night henceforth until the girl is found. When that Dread of the deep night is abroad, let's see where an inch of space would be found for lawlessness. That girl must be produced alive.

Oyidi'a and Orimili Obiora: Ise-e!

[Akaeze gets up heavily takes a few slow steps away]

Akaeze: Times like this make me feel like I have failed the Great One. If his son was seated this very moment on that empty throne, I would gladly gather my rags for the homeward journey.

[Oyidi'a goes to his side]

Oyidi'a: Akaeze, please don't bring tears to my eyes. What have we not done to find the missing prince? Short of taking a fight to the home of the sprits, you and I have played our human part. And we are still doing everything we can.

Akaeze: It's been a painful wait, a search of many years that has drained my patience. I pray to the gods that it won't be like that for this little girl, Uzoma. I want to see her smiling face latest tomorrow morning.

[A wailing is heard outside. Enter a wailing Nnenna, Ugochi following]

Nnenna *[wailing]*: Oyidi'a, mother of all, see what they have done to your daughter. See what they have done to me . . . .

[Oyidi'a rises and hugs the sobbing woman]

Orimili Obiora *[drawing Ugochi aside]*: Why, Ugochi? I told you to manage her.

Ugochi: She insisted and how could I stop her? I had to follow. *[She hurries off to join her fellow women]* Oyidi'a, we come in sorrow.

Nnenna *[wailing louder]*: They have rendered me naked . . . knocked me insane. They have forced open my hand and wrenched from me the joy that heaven put in my hand. Oyidi'a, I am lost, I am lost!

[The three women huddle together]

Akaeze: The crying must stop because the girl is not dead.

Nnenna: If they kill her, I am finished.

Akaeze: Nobody dares kill her. Though moon and sun turn black as soot, that girl must be found alive. It is not a mere wish. It is an order from the royal throne of Umudimkpa.

[Lights dim. Fade]

ACT 3, SCENE 2

Morning at the King's Public Square. Rev. Jones in white soutane is teaching a knot of natives, all standing.

Rev. Jones: Thank you. Daalu nu. Daalu.

Crowd *[amused, laughing]*:   Daalu kwa. *[i.e. Thank you too.]*

Rev. Jones *[pointing at himself]*:   I-I-I!

Crowd [repeating]:   I-I-I!

Rev. Jones *[pointing at them]*: You!

Crowd *[pointing back at him]*: You-uuu!

> *[They repeat the lines thrice, then Rev. Jones applauds]*

Rev. Jones: Clap for yourselves. Clap for yourselves!

[A pregnant woman joins the clapping and shouts "Kua nu aka! Kua nu aka!" (i.e. "Clap your hands!")]

Rev. Jones *[echoing excitedly]*: Kunaaka, kunaaka!

> *[Someone shouts "kusienu aka ike!" i.e. "Clap harder."]*

Rev. Jones: Kusinakike! Very good, very good. Kusinakike!

[Rev. Jones makes some quick entries in his notebook and replaces it on the wooden box]

Fat woman: Anyi asuba kwa oyibo! [See us speaking the white man's language!]

[There is general excitement. Rev. Jones raises a hand and the clapping stops]

Rev. Jones: We are now going to learn counting. *[He spreads the fingers of his left hand and proceeds to count with the right index finger]:* One . . . . Two . . . . Three . . . .

[He repeats the count a few times and gets the people to join]

Crowd: One . . . . Two . . . . Three . . . .

Rev. Jones: What is one in Ibo?

[No one understands the question. He tries various signs, saying one . . . Ibo, one . . . Ibo? till someone shouts "ofu!"]

Rev. Jones: One—ofu

Crowd: One – Ofu!

Rev. Jones: Two?

Crowd: Two—abua!

Rev. Jones: Three?

Crowd: Three—ato!

[Rev. Jones writes in his note book and resumes the class]

Rev. Jones: One—ofu!

Crowd: One—ofu!

Rev. Jones: Two—abua!

Crowd: Two—abua!

Rev. Jones: Three—ato!

Crowd: Three—ato!

Rev. Jones: Kunaaka! Kunaaka!

[The people clap happily]

Rev. Jones: Let's do it this way. Kunaaka One! Kunaaka Two! Kunaaka Three!

[He leads them to clap once, twice, thrice at his say-so. The motion is repeated, everyone is thrilled. Enter four sons of Iwobi bearing their gaunt and emaciated father on a bamboo bed. They place the sick bed beside the white man's tent and step back in silence.]

Iwobi *[croaking with obvious pain]:* Leave me . . . . here with him. Let me . . . die. Let me . . . . die and go. And . . . may it . . . . please . . . the gods!

Umeji (Third son) *[Tearfully]:* You will not die, father. You are innocent and we know it.

Nnaeto (Fourth son): My brothers can go home. I'm staying here with you.

Obinna (First son): None of us will stay back. *[Shooing his brothers toward the exit]* Let us go.

Umeji (Third son): How can we leave him like this?

Obinna (First son): We must obey his wishes. He is our father.

Iwobi *[rasping painfully]:* Go . . . go . . . Find Uzoma . . . Find . . . your sister . . . for me.

Obinna: We will bring her to you, father. It is a promise.

[Rev. Jones leaves his class and walks over, greatly concerned]

Osita: Who can speak the white man's language, let him inform him for us that this is Iwobi, the man he called a witch. He must not delay killing him now, but he must eat his flesh after. *[He gathers a handful of dust and throws it in the air.]* If there is still something in this soil, let it speak and fight for an innocent man!

[As they head out, Rev. Jones calls after them in vain.]

Rev. Jones: Hello, hello there! Hello, a word please. *[Stands, pondering the sick man. Enter Ebili]*

Ebili: When the battles of life reduce a warrior
            To a bamboo bed of rags and common dust
            Who would perceive in such a fevered stub
            The fabled general of yesterwars?
            Who would believe the tingling tale of trophies won,
            The conquest of heights that kissed the skies,
            The single breathe-out that quenched roaring flames
            And took captive monsters of yore with spoils that spun
                                                    legends?
            I weep for Iwobi for death is kinder than this pathetic
                                                    sight.
            Here lies a man, famous in his day; he tapped the
                                                    sweetest wine
            The tallest palms gave him their juicy flows like water
                                                    streams
            His fountains ran at royal feasts and princes drank of
                                                    his delight
            His days and nights fetched springs of life
            To weary troops and drooping herds,
            He recharged the waning moon and dying sun in every
                                                    man
            And gave liver to songbirds and laughter to birdsongs

Now lies he here in public spite
A sorry piece no one would buy,
A sour whisper in the ear
A bitter story in the mouth

[Enter Oche-ilo-eze]

Oche-ilo-eze: What again? Who brought that bed here? And who is that one?

Ebili: That man would need no introduction if the spirits in this land still knew their own best friends. That is Iwobi.

Oche-ilo-eze: I have no patience for your rambling talk. Who brought him here?

Ebili: People who believe he is innocent of what the white man said of him. Oche-ilo-eze, we must find that interpreter. Let's do something to find him.

Oche-ilo-eze: What is your own business with the interpreter? I hear you've gone about telling people that you know him.

Ebili: Not true, not true at all. I said I feel I know him but I can't tell who he is or where or when we met. I know that sounds like I am drunk but I know when I am not drunk. What bothers me is that he knows Apiti. I want him to tell us what he knows about Apiti.

Oche-ilo-eze: Which Apiti?

Ebili: There is only one creature that ever rejoiced in that name. Many, many years have passed but it is still like yesterday. The revolting odour of his last droppings here can never be washed away or wished away. Only Apiti is Apiti.

Oche-ilo-eze: What has that name got to do with what is boiling now?

Ebili: Everything, Oche-ilo-eze! We've all wished hard to forget that horrid past; but can things ever be the same again? Apiti destroyed the crown prince of this land and the throne has stayed hung for twenty years. Apiti almost pushed Umudimkpa into war with Umuachala, something that never happened in all the ages. Apiti attempted to kill the entire council of high chiefs in one sitting. Apiti-

Oche-ilo-eze: Stop invoking that name in this place. It is cursed. The bearer was doomed in life and you must leave his bones to rot now that he is dead.

Ebili: Who is sure he died? He vanished like an evil smoke but that is no proof that he will not resurface some day. The dancing women sing in their songs that seven kinds of death would not be enough to avenge the misery he caused us. That is why I say, let us question that interpreter. He is the only stranger who has mentioned that name in all these years.

Oche-ilo-eze: Ebili, you may refill your calabash as many times as you wish, but take this advice. Leave the interpreter out of your talk. Leave him to your betters.

[Rev. Jones, harried, walks to and fro, kneels by the sick bed. Iwobi glares at him truculently]

Rev. Jones *[praying]:* Almighty Father, our God most loving and merciful, here is a man who at this hour needs your love, mercy and power in a very special way . . . .

[Eyes closed in fervent prayer, Rev. Jones reaches out to touch the sick man. Iwobi reacts]

Iwobi *[shrieks in pain and anger]:* Don't . . . . You . . . Beast!

Rev. Jones: Oh, Father, he needs your touch . . .

[Panting from exhaustion and evident pain, Iwobi draws on a last ounce of strength and spits full in Rev. Jones' face. An instant uproar divides the watching crowd, some faulting Iwobi and others rooting for him. Rev. Jones coolly wipes his face with a handkerchief from his pocket]

Oche-ilo-eze *[gasping in disbelief]:*   A spit! On the white man's face!

Ebili: Before my two eyes or it never happened.

Oche-ilo-eze: Such an affront . . . but why? Why?

Ebili: Affront has two faces, sometimes; and the first to mind is the one behind.

[About to resume his interrupted prayer, Rev. Jones notices the sick man's laboured breath. In a sudden spasm, jerking and kicking, Iwobi slumps down from his sick bed. Rev. Jones runs for a bowl of water and a hand towel; he begins to sponge Iwobi's fevered body, mopping beads of sweat and praying under his breath]

Rev. Jones: Heavenly Father, I plead for this sick man, that he may live and not die. In justice remember mercy; for, if you regard iniquity, no man can stand. Confirm your word this day, the promise you made us that in your name we shall lay hands on the sick and they shall recover . . .

Ebili: He is making his incantations and Iwobi can no longer talk back. Iwobi is dying. Ewo! He is dying . . .

Oche-ilo-eze: There is power in the sacred soil of this square. It shames any evil doer who puts on a bold face to his misdeeds!

Ebili: Iwobi, great tapper, is this the end? You who surveyed the wonders of this world from the tallest palms, you who held daily consultations with the gods up there and came down with pots of goodness for all the world—Iwobi, pride of Umudimkpa, stalwart of the strongest noon, you who poured palm wine as men pour common water—don't let it end like this.

Oche-ilo-eze: All we owe the dead is a mourning and burial. If he is gone, he is gone . . . .

[Lights dim. Fade]

ACT 3, SCENE 3

Late night at Ajofia's obi. The three native policemen are talking in hushed tones, huddled close, seated on the mud bench against a side wall.

Constable 1:   My mind is telling me that we made a bad mistake. This thing is not good. We should not have done this at all.

Constable 2:   Which one?

Constable 1:   The whole thing. We tied up the white man—a whole white man! And we come to hide in a juju man's house.

Constable 3:   I will do anything Abadinegwo tells me to do; I don't want to die like a fowl.

Constable 1:   Still, it is very, very dangerous to close our eyes and ears and just believe that somebody else is thinking for us.

Constable 2:   Stop talking like that. Oga Abadi is our only hope.

Constable 3:   He knows the power of this people and he is a friend of D.O.

Constable 1 *[nervously]*: I think we should stop talking. This place is bad.

Constable 3:   We can talk here as we like. They don't understand our native tongue.

Constable 1:   I'm not talking about humans. I'm worried about spirits.

Constable 2:   Human talk is what keeps away the spirits.

Constable 1:   I never heard that. How do you know?

Constable 2:   I grew up near a shrine. Fear lived with us. We learnt to fight it by talking to ourselves.

Constable 1:   No man can fight spirits.

Constable 2:   If Oga Abadi did not come to our side, where would we be now?

Constable 3:   Hiding in the bush. Or packaged in a smoked basket!

Constable 2:   More like the smoked basket. These people are vicious. How could we face them without guns?

Constable 3:   They would have captured us like small chickens. Where is Corp'l? He went to ease himself and no one saw him again. If Abadi did not come to us, we are bush meat!

Constable 1:   What about the lie we told? It is cheap and childish. I fear what will happen if they find out.

Constable 3:   What are you talking about?

Constable 2:   About the angry bees?

Constable 1:   Yes. Which angry bees?

Constable 2:   It was Abadi's idea and in my own mind, I think it is good.

Constable 1:   A lie is a two-edged sword.

[A sound is heard. They panic and listen awhile, glance at one another and seem to realize that there is no threat]

Constable 3:   When a lie works, why complain? Oga Abadi is very clever.

Constable 1:   Or the people are very stupid. I'm surprised that they could actually believe a blatant lie like that one.

Constable 3:   You too would have believed if you did not know. It takes a big lie to blow the minds of people. If there was no junk story, no one would take us serious.

Constable 2:   I wonder why bros is complaining. The story worked very well didn't it?

Constable 3:   It landed us in safety here. We are getting food with plenty of meat and palm wine. For me, Oga Abadinegwo is the man.

Constable 2:   Even D.O. is always praising him. The man is a genius.

Constable 1:   My body is still itching. We rubbed those biting weeds on our bodies to make the story look real. I'm still itching badly.

Constable 3:   If you use the juju man's oil as he showed us, it will stop completely.

Constable 2:   Mine stopped with common palm oil. I don't know why bros is still complaining.

Constable 1:   We are hiding like bats. We come out only in the night. Even at that, we can't go beyond this compound. It is three nights now. How do we know what they are planning to do to us?

[At another sound, they freeze and look at each other. 2nd constable gets up, tip-toes around peering here and there]

Constable 2 *[returning to his seat]*: Nobody.

Constable 1 *[nervously]*: Juju place. It's like an evil bush. Shouldn't we really keep silent?

121

Constable 2:   Silence is more terrible in a place like this.

Constable 1:   This place is giving me the shakes!

Constable 3:   If you prefer to go back to Ubulu, why not go now and report yourself? Tell them why we are not guarding the man we are supposed to guard. Tell them also that we can't find Corp'l.

Constable 1:   Look, I'm not being childish. I am trying my best to stop worrying, but . . . my mind is telling me that something will go wrong. This Abadinegwo, what do we even know about him?

Constable 2:   What do you want to know about him?

Constable 1:   Look, it is only three months or so that he came to Ubulu. But now, everywhere is full of him. People like that are dangerous.

Constable 3:   See how you put yourself in mud that can bring you down! Who doesn't know that Oga Abadi is D.O.'s good friend? It is true he is very new but D.O. doesn't use him to play.

Constable 2:   It must be a very powerful juju that he fed that man. D.O. just likes him like they are from the same mother.

Constable 1:   A common court messenger only a few weeks ago but overnight, he is head over everybody.

Constable 2:   Me, I don't envy anyone because a man's destiny is marked on the palm of his hand and you can never rub it off.

Constable 3:   I remember how he took over, straight—just like that. From that day that Mr Waribo bent over like this and died. That is how Oga Abadi began to interprete for D.O.

Constable 2:   Now, they go everywhere together. He has completely replaced Mr Waribo. What nobody in this world thought possible but see, it has happened!

Constable 3:   The man is just going up and up, I tell you. Anything he asks me to do I will do it for him.

Constable 1:   I worked with Mr Waribo when he was alive. That time, we enjoyed plenty; plenty—chop, drink, everything! He too was clever—he always took from the natives and he gave us our share. But he just died suddenly that day—just like that.

Constable 2:   His own story has ended. That is how life goes. Let's talk about ourselves.

[Enter Abednego]

Abednego: See, my men, a whispered talk is like a covered banquet. Invited or not, I love to partake.

[All three stand at attention]

Constable 3:   Oga Abadi!

Constable 2:   Shon!

Constable 1:   No complain' sir!

Abednego: Relax, my men. Relax. Sit down, sit down. *[He sits with them]* What were you talking about? See, I know you are worried. But, hear it from me again, you have nothing to fear, nothing at all. Everything is under control. Trust me always.

Constable 3:   We are happy Oga Abadi.

Abednego: You will be happier. I am going to make sure D.O. promotes all three of you.

[All three spring to their feet, preening]

Constable 2:   Shon sah!

Constable 3:   Oga Abadi!

Constable 1:   All correct sah!

Abednego: Relax, my men. You are my friends. I will take you up, up, up. But you must trust me.

Constable 3:   Oga Abadi!

Abednego: Even this work that you are doing, this police life so full of danger, I will do something for you, something that even your own fathers cannot do for you. But if you want it, you must trust me.

Constable 3:   We trust you, Oga Abadi. I trust you with my life!

Constable 2:   Help us, Oga Abadi.

Abednego: Because you are my friends, I will help you. The white man knows many things but he does not know one most important thing—and it is good that every black person knows it, even infants born yesterday. That is what you need most in this dangerous job.

Constable 1:   Juju power?

Abednego: Yes, juju power. Some people are very foolish. Because of white man they say juju has no power. That is why some people die like rats. Your job is very dangerous. You must fortify yourselves the right way.

Constable 3:   Oga Abadi, this is good talk. It is nice to see a senior man like you believing like us.

Abednego: I won't deceive my friends like my fellow big men are always doing. They don't want small people like you to grow like them, that's why. But I know their tricks. There is strong juju, let nobody fool you. Juju is there, strong enough to parboil a man against death! You become strong like a bull and fearless like a leopard . . . and no metal can enter your body! That is what the big, big men are using in the big city and they will never tell you!

Constable 2: We hear about it.

Constable 3: But they say it is very expensive.

Abednego: I will arrange it for you here and you will pay nothing for it!

[The three fall on their knees before Abednego]

Constable 2: Please help us, Oga Abadi. We will never forget you.

Constable 1: People don't know the dangers we face. They don't even remember that we are family men with wives and children.

Constable 3: I am the only male child of my mother. Help us Oga Abadi.

Abednego: Just trust me. I am going to arrange it for you as soon as possible. Get up, get up. You are my friends. I will take you up, up, up! Just trust me.

Constable 3: I will do anything for you, Oga Abadi. Anything you want.

Abednego: I don't want anything from you, my dear friend. If I want anything, I tell the D.O. He is my personal friend and you all know I am working with him. I never worked for that Rev. Jones before and I don't want him again because of this thing he did to you. I am going to have a serious talk with the D.O. about that when we get back to Ubulu.

Constable 3:   Thank you very much, Oga Abadi.

Constable 2:   Oga Abadi, this is not empty talk. From now on, anyone who wants to remove a hair from your head will have to kill us first.

[He quickly whispers into Constable 3's ears]

Constable 3:   Oga Abadi, this juju power, can we get it tomorrow?

Abednego: I am meeting with the big chiefs this night. They will soon be here. We shall see, we shall see!. Let's go and have ourselves a few cups of palm wine before they arrive.

Constable 1:   Oga Abadi!

[Exeunt Abednego and the three constables. Light dims. The cracked voice of Ajukwu, the dreaded masquerade of deep night, salutes in the distance. Enter Ajofia. He walks round the hut, speaking to various objects in the semi darkness]

Ajofia: Ayii . . . .ayiii . . . .ayiiii! Arobilinagu, ageless one that dwells in the no-man's land, you are my eye and ear in my going and coming. Eat your kola. Ochempu, you who defend against shame and dishonor, have your own kola. Aka Ntiji Ani, the hand that breaks the sod, this day's job is done. Oti gbulu gbulu, fighter who beats up my opponents to a pulp, those who reject our terms of peace shall eat the dust of defeat and dismay. Behold, I take my sacred seat in my own homestead. Ajukwu, the masquerade of darkness is up; he presides over the night and none can grudge him. The mention of my name is still ringing loud in melody; I await a tryst with fellow greats in this hut. It is all for the good of the land.

[Ajofia head-bowed relives his moment of honour at the palace as the out-field singing refloats]

Singer/Chorus *[alternately]*:   Ajofia, do-o, do-odo
                                       Ajofia, do-o, do-odo
                                       Ajofia do-o, do-odo
                                       Ajofia do-o, do-odo
                                       Oke mmanwu igbanite?
                                       Ajofia do-o, do-odo
                                       Nnukwu mmanwu igbalute?
                                       Ajofia do-o, do-odo

Singer: Onye g'etu ugo ga ete awa mme n'isi o!

Chorus: Ayeeeh, dike n'ukpo
                Ayeeeh, dike n'ukpo
                Ayeeeh, Ajofia n'ukpo
                Ugo ejugo kwa y'isi o
                Ayeeeh Ajofia n'ukpo loooh! Ooooh!

Ajofia *[aside]*: The smoke that enters the eye and draws tears from it did not set out to meet the eye. The soft mound of shit on the bush path does not complain of trampling feet; it is the person who puts his foot in it that goes howling and cursing. Hear me, Earth and Sky, Sun and Moon. Festivity for lions is funeral for antelopes; so is the truth of all celebrations. Vulture's wife is pregnant and he has considered all the tragic possibilities. But he refuses to mourn any, for if the outcome is a miscarriage, that is a stark breakfast; if the missus dies in labour, she makes a gruesome dinner; if both mother and child be dead, they turn out a whopping lunch. The biggest turns of life leave nothing to chance. It is decision time for this kingdom. The ancient questions must be asked—this time without sentiments.

[Enter Dikeogu and Mmanko. They greet their host wordlessly by raising clenched fists, then unfold their goatskins on the mud bench and sit down]

Mmanko: Ajofia, greetings. We have the girl, but it is impossible to bring her out. The royal hunters are still everywhere and Ajukwu has seized the night. Getting here was not easy.

Dikeogu: This night is clearly unkind to our enterprise. Because of Akaeze, eyes are wide awake and prying that should be deep in sleep.

Ajofia: I have been thinking about it myself. We don't have much of a choice. We have to shift it to tomorrow.

Dikeogu: But the five slaves from my stable have been in your back quarters since noon. Why not do the slaves tonight and the virgin girl later?

Ajofia: That cannot be. The live offerings must be paraded together at the Agbala shrine. Let's sleep over the matter tonight. By tomorrow we must have a perfect plan.

[A slight clap at the door is repeated. Enter Abednego. He removes his hat, showing his heavily bandaged head]

Abednego *[kneeling]*:   Exalted fathers, my knees are on the floor. I just want to inform you that I am ready if you need me.

Mmanko: Rise up, worthy son of our good daughter. It is tomorrow it will happen. This very tomorrow.

Abednego: Please don't feel I am being too forward. You are my fathers, so I must be truthful to you because this thing we are about to do must not fail. I need a big help from you and failure to speak out is a fault of the mouth which may be harmful to the whole body. Let me say it in plain words, as talking to my own fathers: I am scared deep inside. I am very, very scared.

Dikeogu: Fear is a monster that eats up a weak heart. Deal with it or it will deal with you.

Mmanko: An offspring of Umudimkpa cannot talk of fear. It is forbidden. Umudimkpa swallows fear at sight!

Abednego: Great fathers, you chiefs can fight any battle because you have been imbued with powers beyond other mortals. We are about to challenge the white man. My own part in the matter cannot be done with empty hands. It is like putting my head in the mouth of a lion. The white man is a spirit. I need the ancient powers to make him do what I say. Make me the champion spirit of this kingdom, so I can use my position to finish the white man for you.

Ajofia: That one is a small matter. Rise up, fetch that little stool and come over here.

[The misty shape of Mgbafor appears in the opposite corner. Dikeogu is staring vacantly]

Dikeogu *[hoarsely]*:   Mgbafor again. Mgbafor . . .

Ajofia: You see her again?

Dikeogu: She stood there just now. But she's gone away. She's trying hard to tell me something; I can feel it but I don't get it.

Ajofia: Tomorrow, she will rest.

Dikeogu: If there was any doubt in my heart, I would be elsewhere.

Mmanko: All will be calm again. The ancient question settles all spirits.

[Ajofia sits Abednego in the centre, gathers a few things from the rack and beckons on Mmanko and Dikeogu to join him. They surround Abednego as Ajofia ministers]

Ajofia: One addicted to embracing does not go hugging mud
                                          walls
            One who strikes at everything does not punch a mound
                                          of shit
            I summon the four market days to bear witness
            Our son shall be the brightness of the risen sun
            The floods cannot mate the sky; the raging waters
            cannot drown a shining star
            You shall be great as elephant, wise as cobra
            Swift on the hill as antelope, fearless as lion
            Whoever you pursue shall fall
            Whoever pursues you shall fall
            The tongue that speaks good will feast on your name
            The one that speaks bad of you shall not find water

[Ajofia taps him here and there with a handy palm frond, then dabs his head and body with ground white chalk]

Ajofia: You may add your affirmations, Dikeogu.

Dikeogu: Further words are surplus. Let mandate work with power, and power with mandate.

Ajofia: Ise-e! Your turn, Mmanko.

Mmanko *[laying hands on Abednego's head]*:   Your voice must be sweet in the ears of the white man and his people. When you call him, his heart will answer you like a faithful dog. If you ask him to do anything, he will do it and never leave anything out.

All: Ise-e!

[Ajofia lifts up a flat grinding stone from the corner. He lugs it thrice around Abednego's head]

Ajofia: The power of our forefathers to conquer and crush all enemies.

All: Ise-e!

[Ajofia breaks a lobe of kolanut and chews one half, pushing the other into Abednego's mouth. He fetches a small calabash, takes a mouthful of its content and blows sprays in the four corners. He holds the calabash to Abednego's mouth for a tentative sip, then a gulp]

Ajofia: You can now climb any mountain or valley. Fear is now
              afraid of you.

          [Abednego kneels in gratitude, then springs to his feet]

Abednego: Emotions turn my head like a full bottle of nje-nje! I feel
              like the masquerade of my mother's people.*[sings and
              Mmanko choruses: 'Imago mmuo d'ifaa!' (i.e. Do you know
              this masquerade, who he is!)]*

              Abednego/Mmanko *[alternately]*:
              Okoko, Okoko saa iyoo
              Imago mmuo di ifaa?
              Okoko, Okoko saa iyoo
              Imago mmuo di ifaa?
              Akataka nya na agu gbalu mgba
              Imago mmuo di ifaa?
              Otokilika ka obu
              Imago mmuo di ifaa?
              Eziokwu, otokilika ka obu
              Imago mmuo di ifaa?

              "Okoko, Okoko respond
              Any idea what spirit is this?
              Okoko, Okoko respond
              Daredevil that tangled with the leopard
              A veritable monster is he
              Indeed, a real monster is he!"

          [Abednego prances and prowls, lunging at imaginary foes]

Mmanko: *O k'oji me!* That's the deal! That's the sure deal, son of leopards, that's the deal!

Abednego: It is me, it is me! Wind that trap cannot hold! Evil Dog that roasts his head to warm his body! Evil Child who entered his mother's womb from the alleyway!

Mmanko: Contain it! Leopard that pursues antelopes, contain it!

Abednego: Who in this world can stop me now? A child mandated to steal by his own father, what do you expect? Bare-footed kicks to bring down any door!

[He leaps here and there and exits with a jubilant whoop]

Ajofia: There goes a scorpion for the white man's buttocks.

Dikeogu *[pensively]:* I hope we have not created a monster that we ourselves cannot stop.

[A rap on the door . . . repeated. Egbuna's voice]

Egbuna *[within]:* Father, I know it is late. But this cannot wait.

Ajofia: Enter, son.

[Enter Egbuna, with two eldest sons of Iwobi]

Egbuna: Father, my friends come with me—Obinna and Osita, sons of Iwobi. Pardon the breaches. They have an emergency.

[Obinna and Osita fall on their knees]

Obinna: Ajofia, Evil Forest that swallows the terrible, I am on my knees. Our father, Iwobi—you know how it is with him, why he cannot come by himself, he has sent us with kola and strong drink to entreat on his behalf. He says to tell you that strange waters are about to drown him and his household.

Ajofia, you are the visible power of the mighty gods. We come in the depth of night to plead for your help . . .

Osita: My little sister, Uzoma, an evil force has carried her away. My father pleads for her life. *[His voice breaks]* What did we do to anybody to deserve this blow?

Obinna: We need your help, Ajofia, father of all. Mmanko, Sharp Machete that Slays in One Cut, meeting you here is by the hand of the gods. Five good times at your house we couldn't see you.

Mmanko: About this whole thing, I feel too bad. I feel very, very bad. It is that foolish white man at the king's square!

Ajofia: Rise up, my sons. Rise up. Your father did well to send you. Kola and drinks, I will accept—just so you don't feel offended. Gifts never turn their backs once presented to royalty. *[He takes the gifts and puts them on the rack]* Your petition is in order but we are more concerned than you can ever guess. Dikeogu, is it not the very reason we are meeting so late into the night?

Dikeogu: That white man must leave that place. We are sending him off to the evil forest!

Ajofia *[to Obinna and Osita]:* You have seen with your own eyes that we are not sleeping on the matter. But let me hear this. Have you consulted any oracle?

Osita: Yes, we've made enquiries for life and wisdom. They tell us that my sister is still alive and that where she is being held is not very far from her father's compound. That is what we find very puzzling because we have searched everywhere.

Mmanko: My men have not rested since morning. They are the ones leading the search itself.

Obinna: The oracles warn that the girl's life is in serious danger. Her captors intend to kill her in the full moon for a powerful sacrifice.

Ajofia: Leave everything in our hands, then. And consult no further. There is a drumbeat in my ears but not for mere mortals!

Obinna: Ajofia, you are the father we see standing. My family will never forget your help to us in this moment of trial.

[Osita sinks to his knees, singing. Obinna and Egbuna kneel with him and chorus]

Osita: Ajofia, dulu nu anyi pua na mbala
Egwu nsi n'atu anyi o
Chorus: Ijele!
Osita: Ajofia n'efuru mu o
Chorus: Ijele!
Osita: Umudimkpa, kwenu Ijele ekwue

Chorus: O ude egbunam o
Udem egbunam o!

Osita: Ukwu n'atomu n'ije egwu
Onyedu ka mu n'ekpelu asalu aka
Ajuju egbunamu na mu julu ya
Ajofia, n'efuru mu o

Chorus: Ijele!

Osita: Umudimkpa kwenu Ijele ekwue

Chorus: O ude egbunam o!
Udem egbunam o!

Ajofia, kindly lead us forth into the open grounds
Fear of spiritual mines and missiles is upon us
Amazing!

Ajofia, I am lost
Amazing!
Umudimkpa, proclaim this amazing spectacle
May fame not destroy me
May my fame not destroy me!

My feet are stuck on the dance steps
To whom am I to report or complain
An enquiry should not kill me for enquiring
Ajofia, I am lost
Amazing!
Umudimkpa, proclaim this amazing spectacle
May fame not destroy me!
May my fame not destroy me!

[Ajofia seated in glory, raises a horsetail flywhiskacknowledging their solicitations. Ajukwu is heard in the distance, mouthing blood-chilling esoterics in the cracked metallic voice of the ancestral spirits. Lights dim. Fade]

ACT 4, SCENE 1

Early morning at the King's Public Square at Umudimkpa. Rev. Jones comes out of his tent, sneezing. He yawns and stretches, then walks over to Iwobi's tent and kneels by his bed side.

Rev. Jones: Hope you managed to get some sleep, sir? Ooh, now I see you wet yourself. I'll get some water and clean you up.

[He fetches a hand towel and a bowl of water, covers Iwobi's loins with a large towel and beneath it removes the soiled loin cloth. He then proceeds to clean him up with the hand towel. Iwobi's third son, Umeji appears quietly and without a word picks up the soiled cloth.]

Iwobi: You . . . disobeyed . . .

Umeji: Father, how could I leave you all night, alone in this place?

Iwobi: Have . . . they . . . . seen . . . Uzoma?

Umeji: Ajofia has promised to help us. It is you now that everybody is worried about.

Iwobi: This . . . . son of . . . a white . . . . person . . .

Umeji: I hid very well and watched him all night. I had a big pestle. I would have clubbed him to death if he tried any wicked thing on you.

[Enter Ebili]

Ebili: I was watching too. Ogbuefi Iwobi, I greet you.

Iwobi: Whose . . . voice?

Ebili: It is I, Ebili N'atu Ugbo, The Storm that Rocks the Boats. Ogbuefi Iwobi, I am a happy man this morning. Last night,

136

I was much afraid when you fell off your bed. I thought you were dead.

Umeji: My father will not die a death of guilt.

Ebili: That is my prayer too. Ogbuefi Iwobi, I was here last night when you spat on the white man. I thought he deserved worse and I felt very proud of your courage. But this morning, I am feeling very different, after seeing what he did all through the night for you. I have seen that this man is not our enemy at all.

Umeji: I too am confused. Only a brother will do these things he is doing for my father.

[They watch Rev. Jones anoint and massage Iwobi with olive oil. All the time, he prays quietly, totally absorbed with the sick man and battling with his own respiratory condition, his body wracked with occasional sneezes]

Ebili: I lost count how many times he got up to do this last night.

Umeji: More than seven times, and he prayed all the time.

Ebili: At first I thought he was rendering his witchcraft incantations. Later, I realized it was prayer he was saying for your father. I don't know his words but I could feel his heart. This is a good man, Umeji.

Umeji: But I can never forgive him for that terrible accusation. That's what put us in this mess. And now, they have grabbed my sister! Who knows what next?

Ebili: I thought about it all night. I have many questions for the white man but where can we find Abadinegwu, his interpreter? That man must come back here so we can speak our mind to the white man.

[Enter Oche-ilo-eze]

Oche-ilo-eze: I advised you to leave the interpreter alone. He did not tamper with your calabash.

Ebili: He disappeared, Oche-ilo-eze; then all sorts of strange things began to happen around us. I don't know why nobody is seeing what I see.

Oche-ilo-eze: Who else in the whole kingdom carries a calabash as big as yours about?

Ebili: Oche-ilo-eze, I was not looking for compliments. I am only searching for the interpreter. He seems like the proverbial chicken that farted and took off in fear that the entire ground was chasing after him.

Oche-ilo-eze: Ogbuefi Iwobi, greetings.

Iwobi: Greetings.

Umeji: My father is not a witch.

Oche-ilo-eze: If he was, these grounds would have eaten his head before the break of day. I am glad that the King's Square is not polluted by such death. Now you must fetch your brothers and take him home.

Umeji: My father will not leave this place just like that. The white man must tell the whole world with his own lips that what he said about us is not true.

Oche-ilo-eze: Listen, young man. Did you not hear the ekwe reports of the midnight and morning watch? A score of the white man's fighting men are on their way. We don't know what they want but they are armed with loaded rifles.

Umeji: They will meet us here. Maybe they too will help in the search for my sister.

Ebili: The biggest help we need is a mouth that speaks the white man's language and ears that hear it. Your sister will be found.

Iwobi: Oche . . .ilo . . eze . . . .

Oche-ilo-eze: I hear your voice, Ogbuefi Iwobi.

Umeji: My father is saying that his choice is to remain here.

Oche-ilo-eze: When did he tell you that?

Umeji: It is there in his eyes. He says the wind that has blown is a good thing as it has exposed the rump of the fowl.

Oche-ilo-eze: Ogbuefi Iwobi, big words in a child's mouth is not a way to announce the arrival of manhood. I have no quarrel with you or this child. The sons of your father are the ones worrying themselves sick that you are lying here in the open square. I cannot blame them for feeling that way. The shame not felt by a lunatic is endured by his relatives. *[walking away]*

Umeji: No one in his right senses talks like that about my father.

Iwobi: Umeji!

Umeji: I apologise, father. But no one will insult you in my presence.

Ebili: Where is Abadinegwu or is it Abanidiegwu? Nobody is talking about that man. Instead, we are getting angry with one another. Umudimkpa should find Abadinegwu.

Oche-ilo-eze *[turns slowly]*: Stop calling that name . . . .If you know what is good for you, leave the mention of his name out of your mouth.

139

Ebili: I thought we cared about *ofo* and *ogu*.

Oche-ilo-eze: What do you know about *ofo* and *ogu*?

Ebili: Look at these two men—Ogbuefi and the white stranger. Both are victims of what neither knows. Their hearts are full of questions they want to ask each other. But they are separated by a bridge that is not there.

Oche-ilo-eze *[walking away again]*: You are at your rambling talk again!

Ebili: *Ofo* and *Ogu* can never be a rambling talk. That interpreter should be brought here so we can confirm who or what fouled the air. Why punch an innocent head instead of the offending bum for an ugly fart?

Oche-ilo-eze: I will not be taken by your rambling talk. An unthinking head is one with a stinking bum. It is the same nuisance.

Ebili: Every nuisance has a known address, Oche-ilo-eze. The misdeeds of the cockroach should not be blamed on the house rat.

Oche-ilo-eze: Ebili, find a home for yourself. Speaking with you so early in the morning is a bad omen. May this not turn out a confused day for everybody.

[Two middle-aged women are standing by, one carrying an earthenware pot of water, the second a smoking pot of yam potage, on her head. At a signal from Oche-ilo-eze as he heads to the exit, the women deposit the pots beside Rev. Jones' tent. They do a quick general clean-up of the area, picking up a few used utencils for washing]

Rev. Jones: Daalu nu! Daalu nu! (Thank you, thank you all)

1st Woman: Daalu kwa. (Thank you too)

2nd Woman: Nw'onye ocha, daalu. (Thank you, Son of a white fellow)

[Exeunt both women. Rev. Jones hangs some wet cloths on the line, fetches a bowl of water and sitting on his own bed, towels himself. Ebili joins Umeji beside his father's bed]

Ebili *[shaking his empty calabash ruefully]*:   Ah, Ogbuefi Iwobi, my calabash is empty. In the days when the sky poured tides of goodness at a touch of your finger tips, I would be drowning by this time in your waves and torrents of pure delight! I pray you get back on your feet again to mount those palms again. My eyes shall see that day.

Umeji: My father appreciates your goodwill, senior. There are people who now reject palm wine from me and my brothers. They say it is what my father is using to tie up people's good fortune.

Ebili: Your father is a great man. That accusation against him is sad and very unfortunate. I am going to remain here to hear the white man's explanation first hand.

Umeji: My brothers will soon come. One of them will stay over while I go home to freshen up.

> *[The raucous singing of marching troops is heard.*
> *Enter six uniformed native colonial troopers*
> *armed with rifles, marching in twos behind a big,*
> *black sergeant]*

Sergeant and troops *[singing, marching]*:
>   The soldiers march along
>   When they march along in lines
>   They merrily march along in twos and sing a
>   merry song
>   Through to, through to
>   Through to, through to, through to!

The soldiers march along
When they march along in lines
They merrily march along in twos and sing a
                    merry song
Through to, through to
Through to, through to, through to!

[They march to a corner. The sergeant orders them through a quick drill in which they form a single file, turn to face him, present arm and return to full attention. He then strides to Rev. Jones, salutes him and presents a letter to him, standing aside as he opens the envelope and reads]

Voice-over *[from the District Officer, Mr H. Barnsley]:*

Dear Rev. Jones,

I have received very disturbing reports concerning the deteriorating security situation in the Umudimkpa enclave where you have been on a missionary visit in the past few days. Your visit followed my recent assent to your persistent request for clearance to extend your full missionary activities to that area. I had been most reluctant to give that assent, as you may recall, as I had my very serious misgivings based on firsthand intelligence about incipient tensions in the enclave.

Information now reaching my office from assuredly reliable sources has made it clear that this traditionally volatile axis in the Ubulu District of the Native Administration is once again on the brink of anomie, chaos and confusion. This unacceptable development which calls for an emergency action has its needless basis in the protracted leadership crisis engendered by a notorious cabal of aged war lords which has held sway in that enclave for the past twenty years. The self-evident reality of the moment is that peace has broken down and the situation could rapidly degenerate into widespread killings and abductions with dire consequences for governance and trade in the entire Lower Niger region of the Southern protectorate.

I am in close correspondence with the Colonial Office, having given my full assurances that immediate measures are in place and the swiftest steps shall be taken at the District level under my direct charge to nip in the bud all threats to law and order. My instant priority is to restore security and normalcy in these parts, doing so in spite of the daunting challenges, in a manner worthy of the British flag. We shall spare nothing to deliver to these misguided souls the inestimable rights and freedoms guaranteed by Her Majesty, the Queen to all her subjects, dominion, colonial and overseas.

Ahead of an urgent personal visit which I shall presently embark upon, I have sent an advance detachment of troops to the troubled area, and one of the squads will deliver this letter to you. The said squad is under my orders to provide you and your fellow missionaries with on-the-spot defence and protection. I am not unmindful that this arrangement which was unanticipated by either of us might seem like an invasion of your privacy and indeed entail some inevitable inconveniences to your good self. It is my expectation, however, that any reservations you might have about it would be resolved in favour of the larger issues of security for life and property in the context of our colonial experience. I thank you for your understanding and I remain open to a meaningful review of the situation as soon as practicable.

I have the honour to be,

Yours sincerely,
Harvey J. Barnsley,
Ag District Officer.

Rev. Jones: What in God's simple truth does this mean? *[He gets up, scratches his head in evident puzzlement and frustration]*

Sergeant, did you see a fight . . . was there a battle on your way here?

Sergeant: Shon sir! No complain!

Rev. Jones: What exactly is going on here?

Sergeant: Shon sir!

Rev. Jones *[aside]*:   This is ridiculous. What again are they up to?

[Fade.]

ACT 4, SCENE 2

Ajofia's obi in the afternoon of the fourth and last day of Mgbe Dike. Ajofia in ceremonial attire is sitting dejectedly, his wide-rimmed ceremonial head gear of multi-coloured ostrich plumes lying askew on the mud bench against a side wall.

Ajofia: The humiliation is complete. What can be worse? This is supposed to be the last evening of Mgbe Dike. That is the climax point of the festival when every high chief should sally forth to the king's square with *egwu ndi ike,* the dance of war lords. But here is Ajofia, caged in his den. I am prevented from stepping out of my compound. The white man, a mere mortal like us, announces a stoppage of the celebration! then he puts his guns in our face everywhere!

[He rises, paces awhile]

Oche mpu, are you not still there? *Oti gbulu gbulu,* where is your fury? Why is the fusillade of *Amadiora* still in silence? *Agbala,* we have come to the limit, the mocking point for letting things be for too long. The stench is thick in my nose even as a man. So, what about you, the immortals?

[He returns to his seat, tapping a listless foot on the floor]

Ah, rain has beaten the cow straight in the eye! Hear Chiebonam, my head wife. She's even the one leading the noisy lament—like an open revolt in my own back quarters. But who can you blame? Our general docility has turned every man in this land into a eunuch. That is why cockroaches are dancing in the face of the bullfrog; and the dreaded cobra has become a common waist string for the loin cloth of women.

[Chiebonam's voice is heard from the back quarters]

Chiebonam's voice: *Nna anyi* Ajofia, your wives are dressed and waiting. This is our day of pride when like festive eagles, we preen in the spotlight. Are you telling us to undress, strip ourselves of glory plumes? Are we to hang like captive birds or stoop for ever in the shadow of shame? Nkili is here with me, so are Obianuju, Ekwutosi and Nwanyinma and all your daughters are crying.

Nkili's voice: Hear my voice, *Nna anyi*, our patriarch and husband; hear Nkili your wife because she is melting with tears. What will I tell your daughters now? Umudimkpa of my birth and marriage has never taken such a naked slap.

Obianuju's voice: Obianuju refuses to cry. Someone has spat on my face and ordered me not to wipe it. I ask why he did it and he says his name isTerror. I laugh in his face and he is full of angry threats. I am still laughing because he does not know whose wife I am.

Chiebonam's voice: When he gets to know, his feet will yield him wings even if the wind denies him escort.

Ekwutosi's voice: If he does not know, what better time than now to teach him? An albino that dares the blazing sun must suffer a good roasting; then he learns in pain from sores and scars.

Nwanyinma's voice: What exactly are we talking about? When did a mongrel dog gain the fangs of a lion? Who is his father that he can dare to roar back at a leopard? Nwanyinma is here, awaiting your stirring, *Nna anyi*.

Chiebonam's voice: Please let it be just a stirring of your finger, not the full hand of your storm.

Nwanyinma's voice: No, *Nna anyi*, let the storm rage in full blast. Dreadful and deadly let it rage, *Nna anyi*. Certain beasts can never learn any lesson of life except at the funeral of their own kind!

Nkili's voice: Stirring or storm, this is your moment of truth, *Nna anyi*. Whatever you decide, let it happen like bushfire—now or never! Rise and we shall go with you.

Ekwutosi's voice: Is there a death that kills a person twice? A great warrior's wife is a warrior in her own rights. Arise, *Nna anyi*. Let us redeem our pride or the abjects of this world will begin to mock us in whoops and whispers.

Nwanyinma's voice: Today, not tomorrow! Let us confront those rascals! Let's confound them with the boldness of angry bees. Whose sons are they? Let's go out there and mock their guns as toys!

Obianuju's voice: *Nna anyi,* questions are crawling around us like busy ants. The passing moments give steam to the rising buzz of anxiety. What is this thing called terror that is lying on the way? If the war machete of the menfolk is blunt or forbidden, what about the everyday broom in the hands of women? Should the brave hunter recoil into himself to avoid trouble or eat his heart to confront it?

Chiebonam's voice: The great warrior must prove himself in the day of smoke and amulets. Ajofia, *Nna anyi*, the drums have been silenced, but the melody is not ended. The hearts of your wives are beating loud for you . . .

[Ajofia paces]

Ajofia *[aside]*: Goats have grazed on my head! Goats have grazed upon my head!

[Enter Egbuna]

Egbuna: Father, are we going or not? My elder brothers sent me to ask.

Ajofia: Go and tell your head mother, Chiebonam that if I hear one more sound from any of them in that place, it is her head I will severe and offer to the gods.

[Exit Egbuna. Ajofia retakes his seat.
Mmanko's voice is heard approaching]

Mmanko *[within]*:   Aha! Peace of the grave! Aha! What we have been saying for years . . . Aha! has it not happened now?

[Enter Mmanko, very agitated]

Ajofia: Mmanko, goats have eaten fodder off my head.

Mmanko: Those who tell us peace, peace—what are they going to tell us now? When we talk, they think we are foolish. Who is not foolish now?

Ajofia: I don't suppose you heard me, Mmanko. I said goats have eaten fodder off my head.

[Mmanko gets seated]

Mmanko: Who has ever drunk such insult? I was already dancing to the square, in my full regalia . . . all my family behind me. Then, the sons of nobody came with their guns; and they stopped us. I still can't believe it. It is like a bad dream . . .

Ajofia: Mmanko, my people were out there in my forecourt, waiting for me to join them. I was just about to put my head in the crown. They charged into my compound, fired shots and ordered the drumming to stop. In my very presence, they threatened to take my sons and brothers away.

[Enter Dikeogu]

Dikeogu: My own story is no different. One of the idiots threatened to shoot me. I told him that as he pulled the trigger, his father

148

and mother would die back home wherever he came from, and I would still be standing to make him run mad. He apologized after that, he and his team mates. *[Sitting]* I have sent them palm wine to drink, so they don't go bothering my family.

Mmanko: Ah! That is great wisdom. I must do the same when I get back.

Dikeogu: We are now in the real mess of our lives. This is what I warned Akaeze about so many times but he would not listen. I wonder what he would say now.

Ajofia: He can say anything; but of what use? It is the late cry of a man who allowed his eyes to be put out—a man who did not realize that a finger being poked in his face for sport would some day pierce his eye.

Dikeogu: The ekwe announced that the big white man is even arriving today.

Ajofia: He is bringing something evil. That is why he has filled everywhere with guns. And that is why he cancelled our Mgbe Dike. He has conquered us without a fight.

Dikeogu: What is our plan for our plan? Or shall we too bury our heads like ostriches?

Mmanko: Never! No going back!

Ajofia: Yesterday has no return gate, Dikeogu. Tonight the ancient questions shall find answers in running blood.

Dikeogu: The white man has his guns everywhere.

Ajofia: Will the guns shoot what they cannot see? It is a night to slide into the slough and run the *Ajukwu* circuit. *[He stands up abruptly and puts out his open left hand]* Tonight at full moon.

[Mmanko and Dikeogu place theirs on it]

Mmanko: Tonight at full moon.

Dikeogu: Tonight at full moon!

[All three cover the pile with their right hands]
[Re-enter Egbuna]

Egbuna: Father, the leaders of Gosiora and Osilike are here to see you. Words of fire are in their mouths and they refuse to wait.

[Enter Ndukwe and Ifeka]

Ndukwe: Ajofia, great father, we come from an emergency meeting of our two age grades.

Ifeka: Our greatest respect is what brings us here.

Ndukwe: You are the only one still worthy of our consultation. The rest of the chiefs and elders have betrayed our trust and surrendered our heritage to strangers.

Ifeka: We have taken a final decision!

Ndukwe: We die this very night, but shame must be wiped out from Umudimkpa.

Ifeka: Restrain, restrain is all we kept hearing from the elders. First shot hit a brickwall; second shot hit the same brickwall. Third shot has to ask itself whether it is a case of bad shooting or the brickwall is the real target.

Ndukwe: Our patience has run out at last. Tonight, we kill the white man and all his agents in this land.

Ifeka: Tomorrow means nothing from now on. The guns of the white man do not scare us.

Ndukwe: What is about to happen in this land will make ears to tingle all around the world.

Ifeka: Only the hand of Ajofia can stop us now. That's why we have come, Ajofia, father of all.

[A long pause]

Ajofia: Gosiora and Osilike, you offend me. *[Returns to his seat in deep thought]* Mmanko, Dikeogu, please indulge, take your seats awhile.

[Mmanko and Dikeogu sit, woodenly]

Ajofia: You see these two great pillars of the kingdom here with me, and what happens? You disregard them? It is me you insult by that! Would that happen if you knew that Ajofia is Ajofia?

Ifeka: We are sorry but the mandate we bear regards no one but Ajofia himself.

Ndukwe: It was the fancy halts and hesitations of tradition that brought us to the present mess. We must move different to move forward.

[Ifeka kneels, Ndukwe hesitates then joins him]

Ifeka: Gosiora and Osilike are begging you to show your hand before sunset. Only you can save our country now.

Ndukwe: We are pleading, Ajofia. Send your bees. Release the flying fury of our forefathers as you did before.

Ifeka: It has to happen quickly before sunset. It has to be now, before the darkness falls.

Ndukwe: It is a last act of mercy. Your bees will sting the bastards, scatter the white man and his gunmen so we don't have to kill them.

Ifeka: It has to happen before sunset,

Ndukwe   Otherwise, . . . it is the night of blood! Ours and theirs!

Ajofia *[fans himself absent-mindedly for a while]*:
    Mmanko, Dikeogu . . . . these are children of yesterday. They lack wisdom. Do you see what I see?

Dikeogu: You are right, Ajofia. No wise man pours his heart like fuel into an offensive word that another put into his mouth to spit out.

Ajofia: A child that puts his head in the mouth of a lion in the name of mandate, would he ever again speak of mandate?

Egbuna: Father, you are missing the point. *[He kneels with his colleagues]* I am part of this decision and we took an oath to seal it. Tonight we die.

Ajofia: You took an oath!

Egbuna: Yes father, to wipe out everything of the white man. That includes the four men that are hiding in this house.

Ajofia: Did you hear that, Dikeogu?

Dikeogu: It is a fearful thing when boldness combines with ignorance. It begets an ugly type of stupidity that openly delights in suicide. But we must forgive our young men. Have we not been young ourselves? As you rightly said a moment ago, they are only children of yesterday.

Mmanko: Dikeogu has spoken my mind.

[A long pause]

Ajofia: Rise up, young men. *[The young men rise with some reluctance.]* A child who wants to run ahead of his father must be sure of the destination and the secrets of the way . . . Tell me, what do you know of the four men you want to kill?

Egbuna: They work for the enemy but the gods have delivered them into your hands. We need no hostages!

Ajofia: Is this the voice of my son or the echo of a possessed mob? Ajofia must know who is daring him . . . . so as to choose the right weapon!

Egbuna: You still don't get it, father. We who are standing before you are already dead. Tonight, we find our graves; but the enemy shall die first. Umudimkpa must be purged of this shame.

Ajofia: Egbuna, my son, it is not the sender of an insult that has offended royalty but the fool whose mouth delivers it. *[He rises]* The riot inside me at this moment knows neither son nor slave. Don't tempt me to pronounce a curse on your head, or Amadiora will . . .

Dikeogu: Hold it, Ajofia, please hold it. *[He stands]* Don't let anger spill what sorrow will regret.

Egbuna: But isn't that what we are saying? Amadiora should face the white man.

Dikeogu: Shut up, boy! Who are you to spit words at your own father?

Ifeka: We did not come here to fight.

Ndukwe: True; the enemy we are sworn to fight is out there, not here.

Dikeogu: Your impudence makes nonsense of your best intentions. What do you know of what you think you know?

Mmanko: They never ask questions. They just jump up and start doing things! Talking any how!

Egbuna *[aside]:* Blame is sweetest in the mouths of elders because they never speak of their own failures.

Ajofia: What did I hear you say?

Egbuna: You heard me well, father. I will not be alive to see my father slapped in the face by an idiot of any colour!

Ajofia *[angrily]:* Your father can fight his own fights. Did he ask you for help?

Egbuna: My father never asks for help. His sons are there, but they will always be small boys in his eyes—children of yesterday!

Ifeka: Calm down, Egbuna. We cannot afford a fight with your father.

Egbuna: I will never fight my father, but he has to hear the truth. Guess why my elder brothers don't enter this *obi*. They are sick of being treated as infants or strangers. My father will rather die than ask anyone to help him.

Ndukwe: Is that not so with all our fathers? We are children for ever in their eyes. They say we don't ask questions; but do they ever take us into confidence as grown-ups? Strangers see the break in our ranks. Where is the bond of manhood that once made this kingdom tough as the iroko and feared as a loaded gun?

Mmanko: There is too much talk in these children!

Dikeogu: I think there is a point they are trying to make. But do they
           know what it takes to be men at a time like this? I suggest
           that Ajofia should speak a few words into their ears. Let
           them hear a secret or two that should open their eyes. They
           would see that the bond they are talking about is why we
           three are sitting here.

[Ajofia waves them to a seat on the mud form and retakes his own]

Ajofia: It is said that elder cows chew and their young ones watch
           their mouths to learn. It is a curse on this age that our sons
           are neither watchful nor mindful; they are in too much
           haste and think they know it all. Questions they never ask;
           and every good counsel passes through one ear and out the
           other . . . These two high chiefs, you met them here when
           you came in. They are the ones with whom Ajofia borrows
           the eyes of ants to see the path of the spirits. But what do
           you know of that? And why are they here? That is the kind
           of question which you never ask. I have nothing more to tell
           you in words.

Mmanko: Use your tongues to count your own teeth. That is wisdom.

Dikeogu: What Ajofia will not shout to tell you is that this very night,
           something will happen.

Mmanko: A very big thing will happen.

Dikeogu: *Ajukwu* will do what the ancients did in their times. You and
           your mates, if you know what is good for you, stay inside the
           huts; step not outside. That is all you should know for now.

Ajofia: And by the way, let no finger touch my four guests. They are
           the key to things you will hear about.

Mmanko: I am even thinking, let us make them drink an oath of blood. That is how they will not go and harm the son of our daughter.

Ajofia: I agree with that. Imagine their madness! These children would have killed the son of their own sister, the person we need most for the task ahead!

Dikeogu: It boils down to the same fault—they never ask questions!

Ajofia: Egbuna, go there and call the interpreter.

[Egbuna shifts uncomfortably, confers with his mates]

Ajofia: What are you delaying for? Go and call the man. In fact, bring him and his three fellows!

Egbuna: They are not here any more . . . . Our mates found them outside this compound and took them away.

[Everyone is on his feet]

Ajofia: Took them away to where? Egbuna! Where are those men?

Ndukwe: The decision is to kill them tonight if we can't convince you to send the bees.

Ifeka *[hastily]*:   But because of what you told us now, the plan will change. We'll run and persuade our mates to release them.

Ajofia: You brainless goats, let nothing scratch that interpreter!

Dikeogu: Do you even know who he is? You never ask questions.

[Commotion outside: male voices chanting at the doorsteps]

Voices chanting: Mgbe dike egbu mmadu
                     Obu na mgbe dike egbu mmadu n'oma ana

> Mgbe dike egbu mmadu
> Obu na mgbe dike egbu mmadu n'oma ana
>
> If Mgbe dike hasn't killed a man
> If Mgbe Dike hasn't killed a man, it can't be over!

Ajofia *[yelling]*:   Tell those beasts of the wilderness to stop that noise in my house!

[Ifeka darts out, shouts the noisy gang down and re-enters. Achi follows gingerly, a thick pile of hair in his hand]

Achi: See what we found.

Ndukwe: What is that?

Achi: The interpreter's beard.

Egbuna: The interpreter? His beard, how? Where is the man?

Achi: He tried to run away with his men; but he wasn't as lucky.

Ndukwe: The others escaped?

Achi: Yes, but the interpreter was the big fish and look what we got. No one knew his beard was fake!

Ajofia: Let me see that thing.

[It is passed to him. He inspects it by the dim light in the corner. His two colleagues close in to get a view]

Mmanko: Our daughter's son has cunning like a tortoise.

Dikeogu: But I don't get it. Why should a man wear a fake beard?

Ajofia: Maybe a mask to fool the white man.

Dikeogu: Suppose it was meant to fool us?

Ajofia: What does he gain by that? I remember he actually told me that his face was a mask to deceive the white man. Yes, he said those words . . .but I thought it was just a figure of speech.

Dikeogu: The beard made him look like a black copy of the white preacher.

Mmanko: I think it is a clever trick . . . . But these young men have done it again, ah! Never waiting to ask why something is covered, they rush to uncover it. Is it not the same as stripping a masquerade? It is very bad!

Dikeogu: It is important now that we see him very quickly. They should go and bring him now.

Ajofia *[turning to the young men]:* What are you still waiting for? Go now and bring him here! *[Exeunt all the young men. The three chiefs retake their seats. Lights get dimmer]*

Mmanko: The blood is pounding in my head as in the days of battle . . . .when Umudimkpa was Umudimkpa and fear was afraid of us! It will be such a night tonight.

Dikeogu: I sent trusted men outside the kingdom. But they all came back with empty stories. We have no choice about our virgin girl.

Mmanko: Did you need to bother your skin?

Dikeogu: It was one last attempt to spare Iwobi. But his own gods have not helped him

Ajofia: We must be strong to finish what we began. No sentiments. Tonight at full moon!

Mmanko: Tonight at full moon!

Dikeogu: Tonight at full moon!

[*Enter Obinna and Osita. They kneel*]

Obinna: Worthy fathers, please do not think us inconsiderate or importunate. When a man is laden with a burden that is bigger than him, he goes stammering for help.

Osita: My baby sister, Uzoma is still missing. We are filled with fear at the approaching sunset. If something is not done, they may kill her this very night.

[*A long pause. Ajofia ignores them, takes a thing invisible from the shelf and returns to his chair*]

Ajofia: So, you blocked your ears after I told you to stop consulting the oracles? Why should I continue with you?

Obinna: Ajofia, father of all, please don't feel offended. When a man is staggering under a heavy burden . . .

Ajofia: No, no, no! If you think you can handle it better than us, we'll wash our hands off the matter.

Osita [*rising quickly to his feet*]: Please forgive us, fathers. It is not like that.

Obinna [*also rising*]: My father asked us to bring a goat over to you. We have tied it in the back yard. It is to encourage you in what you are doing for us. Please take no offence.

Ajofia: It is your matter that tied us down. Just like a fight between the pit bull and the odd-jobs man, it's a fight to a finish. Is that not evident? Now, go home and leave this matter in my hands. Nothing will happen to that little girl unless her own *chi* has spoken otherwise.

Obinna & Osita: Thank you, fathers. Thank you, Ajofia.

[Exeunt Obinna and Osita. Mmanko turns and exchanges chieftains' handshakes first with Ajofia, then with Dikeogu]

Mmanko: We have killed murmurs and rumours.

[A lone singer is heard outside. Enter Ebili]

Ebili: I bring hefty baskets of greetings, Ajofia, Evil Forest that swallows the monster which swallowed the elephant. I greet you too, Dikeogu, Strongman of Battles fought and yet to be fought, and you Mmanko, Sharp Machete that slays in one cut and positions for another kill. I went to your house, Dikeogu, and I was told I would find you here. I said to myself, be the first to bring the news to Dikeogu and his household. That is what I said to myself and I started running all the way to this place, no, to your place first, then to here. From today, no one will hear what I say and dismiss it as the words of a drunk except he is drunk himself. I am the happiest man in the whole world today.

Ajofia: Who is mocking Umudimkpa with talk of happiness on this day of grief?

Ebili: The mood in the kingdom will pass away when people hear this news. It still sounds unreal to me, but I saw him with my own eyes. I was even the one that recognized him as all those boys were newborn or unborn at the time of his past horrors.

Dikeogu: What is he talking about?

Ebili: When I recognized him and shouted his name, he started playing games to confuse me. But that didn't fool me . . . someone I'd known in all my years of childhood and . . . I never believed any of those stories that he was dead and long buried.

Ajofia: My good fellow, you are talking and not talking. What is your real problem?

Ebili: Problem? It is Umudimkpa that was going to have a serious problem. But something was telling me to watch that man. I told you elders that he was familiar but no one listened to me. They said I was drunk! Did I deny I was drunk? Is it news when I am drunk? He came here with the white man. He said his name is Abadinegwo. Abanidiegwu—and you believed him. But you didn't believe me when I told you that something is wrong. That fellow is the most dangerous person I've ever met in this world.

[The three high chiefs are quick on their feet]

Mmanko: What is he talking about?

Dikeogu: Is it the interpreter? What about him?

Ebili: You should have seen his face without that fake beard. The boys are dragging him to the palace. He is the fake that he has always been, the son nobody wants to call his own. Twenty years ago, he almost wiped out all the high chiefs including his own father.

Dikeogu: Are you out of your mind? What are you talking about?

Ebili: I am telling you what you should thank me to know. And I deserve *oji nwa dike* for saving Umudimkpa from evil. The interpreter is evil! And evil is the interpreter! The man is not what he called himself. He is Apiti!

Mmanko: Which Apiti?

Ebili: The very same Apiti whose name is loud in all the bad songs. The same Apiti who prefers you all dead!

[Fade]

ACT 4, SCENE 3

Evening at the king's public square at Umudimkpa. Rev. Jones in white soutane is seated on a log in front of his tent a few metres from Iwobi's shed. Sitting opposite him on the big wooden box and smoking a big curved pipe is the District Officer, Mr Harvey J. Barnsley, a balding middle-aged man in well-starched khaki shorts and short sleeves, knee-high brown hoses and heavy black shoes. Mr Barnsley has this habit of thumbing his thick stylized mustache from time to time, his cupped fist around his pipe. His free hand cuddles a rimmed colonial hat on his lap.

Barnsley: You talk of God and heaven and that's quite fine with me. But here we are in the heart of a savage jungle. I am the one with a job to do, a job assessed by visible results and cold numbers in revenue and cost of administration.

[At a grunt from Iwobi, Rev. Jones gets up, checks on him quickly and returns to his seat]

Rev. Jones: I am praying for you, sir. Whatever our duties may be, we must show Christian love and fear of God.

Barnsley: Reserve the sermon for the natives. They need it to become good subjects and better tax-payers to Her Majesty's Government.

Rev. Jones: Everybody needs the word of God, especially those who don't think they need it.

Barnsley: Preach to the natives. Make your quickest converts; or it would fall on me to dispatch a few hundreds of them to that place you call hell. Where is my man, Abednego? I need him for a major assignment, the reason I came here.

[Barnsley rises and Rev. Jones follows suit]

Rev. Jones: You obviously have some kind of hand on him, which perhaps explains a few things. I'd be quick to admit to a bit of confusion at the moment. But I'm trying to mind my mission and nothing else.

Barnsley: You preachers share one bad habit with these natives, you know? You speak in parables and roundabouts that arrive at nowhere. That can be an irritant to a busy mind like mine, but don't let that bother you tonight. What do you think of him, by the way? I mean my man, Abednego?

Rev. Jones [*after a contemplative pause*]: How best can I put this now? I could say he knows his ropes. Or better still, he can mind the ropes. [*He checks on Iwobi again and adjusts his pillows*]

Barnsley: You are spot on if by that you mean he is competent and resourceful. I find him extremely focused and self-driven, assertive and eager to get things done. These are very uncommon attributes around here. Besides, he speaks and can read some English—which is what really excites me. It has taken us months but I am confident at long last that we have the right man.

Rev. Jones: Right man for what, sir, if I may ask?

Barnsley [*turns slightly then halts*]: Oh, we mustn't breach official protocol in such matters. The announcement is due shortly. Where is he anyway? I've brought you a replacement, someone more suited for your work—a church type, if you know what I mean. That's the lean fellow standing over there with the porters. Name is Hezekiah.

[*Barnsley points a raised hand in the direction of a knot of attendants in the far corner. Hezekiah, a stringy man in well-ironed white shirt and black shorts bows deeply*]

Rev. Jones: I appreciate your kind gesture and I shall be glad to return the favour as soon as possible. I'll push myself quite hard to bridge that language gulf within a year. I am very passionate about the education programme and it must work.

Barnsley: I wish you all the luck you can find. But I know these natives much better and I wish I could spare you the certain frustrations.

Rev. Jones: What I see are a wonderful people that God has made but communication is the bridge we must build to engage with them. If you ask me, sir, there is no problem here but the dearth of interpreters.

[Barnsley puffs at his pipe, retakes his seat and waves Rev. Jones back to his own seat.]

Barnsley: You see things from the narrow end of your work as a church missionary; and there may be a point in that. But based on the hard facts staring me in the face after months in this jungle, our primitive hosts are—permit me to say—rather like infants.

Rev. Jones: That sounds quite uncharitable, I would think, sir.

Barnsley: I could tell you worse about your natives; and in due course you will thank me for the early tips. They are a curious bunch as you will find out, full of long talk but quite incapable of thinking for themselves. Time and time again, they prove you hopelessly wrong when you expect they could build or sustain the most basic leadership institutions without our help. That is their biggest challenge—from my better informed standpoint surely.

Rev. Jones: Perhaps we should do a little more to understand their situation and their way of life.

Barnsley: No one is stopping you. I certainly don't oppose your dreaming your so-called 4-R programme— Reading, wRiting, 'Rithmetic and Religion. But unlike you clergymen who are answerable to God of Heaven, my administration serves Her Majesty the Queen of England right here on earth. I do not have your privilege to wait or waste a whole century on a little piece of fancy.

Rev. Jones: Well, sir, I reckon we have our different calling. It is a great work that I see before me. But He who has called me is faithful and never fails.

Barnsley [*rising up*]: I have an important meeting with the chiefs. If you wish to go with me to the palace, let's get cracking.

Rev. Jones [*rising too*]: I'd rather stay back, sir, if you don't mind. The work of The King needs me here.

Barnsley [*gruffly*]: Suit yourself. Where is my man, Abednego?

Rev. Jones: Am I to believe that he did not return to Ubulu, sir? He left here three days ago.

Barnsley: I don't get that, Mr Jones. You sent him away?

Rev. Jones: Not at all. He excused himself to freshen up, and that was it.

Barnsley: What about your guards?

Rev. Jones: They too.

Barnsley: And you think that is normal? Wait a minute! Isn't something going on here? You don't see a red signal?

Rev. Jones: What red signal, sir?

Barnsley: You obviously under-estimate these natives. You haven't seen their brutality and you don't seem to know that they are most vicious against their own! My man could be in gravest danger and here you are, not even a thought!

Rev. Jones: I have no fears for him, sir.

Barnsley: You have no fears for him?

Rev. Jones: Not at all, sir. I told you a minute ago, he knows his ropes.

Barnsley: And what exactly do you mean by that?

Rev. Jones: Some pranksters tried to scare me the other night with ropes. He was one of them.

Barnsley: Can you prove that? You saw him face to face?

Rev. Jones: My perfume gave him away, sir. And I saw more telling evidence in the foot prints the next morning—sandals! No one else has them here.

Barnsley: Hmmm! A little riddle on our hands is what it sounds like. But I know my man, Abednego. No quarters given or taken, he is after something big or something big is after him.

Rev. Jones: How do we get to find out?

Barnsley: A visit to the palace straight away. They must produce him immediately or face my full wrath. Are you sure you don't want to come along?

Rev. Jones: Duty calls right here, sir.

Barnsley: I suppose by duty you mean things like that. *[Waves in the direction of Iwobi's bamboo bed]:* How many are you going to bother with?

Rev. Jones: As many as the good Lord brings my way, sir.

Barnsley: Well, good luck as I said before. But remember you are not a licensed physician.

Rev. Jones: I work with the Great Physician, sir.

Barnsley: You've been sneezing from a bad cold. Good job to attend to it, right?

Rev. Jones: Thank you for your concern, sir.

[Mr Barnsley snaps his fingers and four porters trot over with a carriage chair which they set down at his feet. They remain in genuflection as he climbs in, then they heave it shoulder-high and set out with two armed guards in front, two behind, and one on each flank. A solitary patrol stays behind.]

Rev. Jones *[kneeling in prayer]*: O God, our Father in heaven, what are we that you are mindful of us? Overloaded so with privileges we become puffed up with pride and even deny you your place as our Creator! Deliver us from conceits and teach us to number our days lest we perish like the self-accursed . . .

[Enter Oche-ilo-eze, followed by Umeji and a few layabouts]

Oche-ilo-eze *[in evident agitation]*: Those who look for trouble will find it hung around their own necks! The evil they are weaving to put on our shoulders, the fear of it will eat their own heads!

Layabouts: Ise-e!

Oche-ilo-eze: Who do these people think they are? They debarred me from my own premises, the grounds of my forefathers! Pigs carrying rifles forced me out of the square!

Umeji *[kneeling at Iwobi's bedside]*: Father, they insisted I must leave as well. The praying one tried to stop them but they pushed me out with others.

Iwobi: I saw it, son. Don't worry.

[Rev. Jones joins Umeji at Iwobi's bedside. He lays a hand on Iwobi's forehead and mutters a brief prayer.]

Oche-ilo-eze: If the whole world is burning with the sudden fires of a new madness, it is time for a remedy from the ages past. I have in my hand the ash of fury here. I advise everyone to leave the square immediately. I am going to blow blindness and leprosy in the face of the white man. All of you, please clear the square.

Umeji: But this man has done you no wrong. The person troubling us is their chief, the man whose feet are lifted above the ground.

Oche-ilo-eze: If you know what is good for you, move away, all of you. Or you too become lepers!

Iwobi: Oche-ilo-eze.

Umeji: My father is calling you.

Oche-ilo-eze: My ears are not deaf. I said, step back.

Umeji: No, Oche-ilo-eze. This man is helping my father. If you must blow that thing in someone's face, here is mine.

Iwobi: Oche-ilo-eze! Oche-ilo-eze!

Oche-ilo-eze: Is this not the man who accused your father?

Umeji: Hear my father first. He wants to talk to you.

Iwobi: Come, Umeji. Give me your hand. Here, hold my hand, now.

Umeji: See! My father's hand is up! It is up! My father's hand is up! Father!

[Rev. Jones grips Iwobi's hand and gently pulls him to a half-sitting position, wedging his back with pillows. Umeji lends a hand, awed but visibly excited]

Iwobi: Oche-ilo-eze.

Oche-ilo-eze: Ogbuefi Iwobi.

Umeji *[dancing]*:   My father is sitting up. First time in two years!

[Rev. Jones turns into his tent and draws the drapes]

Iwobi: Oche-ilo-eze . . . .

Umeji: My father wants to tell you that . . . .

Iwobi: I will speak, son. I'll speak. I feel a rush of power in my body. Something happened when that man put his hand on my forehead.

Oche-ilo-eze: I am happy to see you sitting up, Ogbuefi Iwobi, and speaking with new vigour in your voice. It confirms that the spirits are not blind to their duty.

Iwobi: Thank you, Oche-ilo-eze. I want us to look each other in the face because my maternal homestead and yours are the same, so if I die in your hands, the cry will not be for me alone. But you will not blow anything in the face of this white man until he answers the questions I have for him. And I will not move from here until I hear what he has to say.

Oche-ilo-eze: Ogbuefi Iwobi, the stubbornness of my mother's people is strong in your head as it is in mine. But you are on sick bed and I should not drag a matter with you.

Iwobi: I appreciate your forebearance, Oche-ilo-eze, though my sickness is not even the issue. It is fear for my daughter's life

169

that has driven me to this point and I am ready to fight even the gods. You must help me bring that interpreter here! I have desperate things to say to my white friend here.

Oche-ilo-eze: The interpreter has become the most coveted bride in the land!

Iwobi: My need for him is most urgent.

[Enter Odikpo, looking agitated]

Odikpo: Oche-ilo-eze! I greet you. Ah! Ogbuefi, it is wonderful to see you sitting! All Umudimkpa must celebrate.

Iwobi: Welcome, Odikpo. My sons told me they borrowed white man's money from you.

Odikpo: That is why I am here. I ran to your house but Obinna wasn't there. I hope he has not given the money yet.

Umeji: Why? The money is to pay the interpreter or he will not meet my father. Obinna has gone to give it to him.

Iwobi: Is there a problem?

Odikpo *(scratches his head thoughtfully):* There is a big problem. The interpreter is not . . . . He is not the interpreter. He is someone else . . . . His name is Apiti.

Oche-ilo-eze and Iwobi: Which Apiti?

Odikpo: The one in all the bad songs.

Oche-ilo-eze: Apiti? Are you sure what you are talking about?

Odikpo: All of us were surprised when his big beard came off like a mask. We didn't know anything until Ebili chanced by and recognized him. The boys are taking him to the palace.

Oche-ilo-eze: Apiti? Apiti! I must see this one with my own eyes!

[Exit Oche-ilo-eze, hobbling off on his long staff]

Odikpo: I have to find Obinna. Please let him know that I came here. I just hope he hasn't parted with the money.

[Exit Odikpo]

Umeji: Father, this person called Apiti, why does everybody hate him so?

Iwobi: Apiti is a bad story, son. He is the evil possibility in every child and the bad peerage a kid must avoid. Help me to turn on my side. My back is aching.

[Two armed guards burst onto stage, yelling orders to clear the square. Rev. Jones emerges instantly from his tent]

Rev. Jones: Hey, not again! Leave them alone! Back off, will you! Leave them alone!

[Re-enter Mr Barnsley on his carriage chair with entourage. He refuses to be set down. The porters shift slowly, humming rhythmically under their load]

Mr Barnsley: Rev. Jones, I over-rule. You are coming with me to the palace.

Rev. Jones: May I understand you, sir?

Mr Barnsley: You have no idea what things were happening under your nose. Are you aware of the spate of abductions?

Rev. Jones: Was anyone abducted, sir?

Mr Barnsley: Your patient over there—his daughter was taken. Then, my man, Abednego went under cover to investigate; and guess what? They kidnapped him too!

Rev. Jones: Under cover you said, sir. I never knew of it.

Mr Barnsley: This is big. Very big! But terrible if I didn't spot that lynch mob on time! I rescued him from them; and now, we can rescue others with his help. Ask your patient about his daughter. Hezekiah, come on, assist.

[Hezekiah bows, chats briefly with an animated Iwobi]

Hezekiah: He is telling thee that his daughter is being stolen and it passing three days. He is not knowing who the stealers are being who. But he is fearing of them if they being with planning to killing the beautiful girl.

Rev. Jones: What is the girl's name?

Hezekiah: They calling her Uzoma, *Door Beautiful.*

Mr Barnsley: I have dispatched troops to rescue her immediately. You won't believe she is being held by one of the so-called high chiefs. Do you know the one called Mmanko?

Rev. Jones: I have him on my to-visit list.

Mr Barnsley: That blighter is heartless! But so is the whole pack, any way. My man, Abednego has gone with the troops to search his house. Come on, Rev. Jones, let's go up to their palace and put a stop to all the mess!

[Lights dim. Fade]

ACT 4, SCENE 4

Throne room at Umudimkpa palace. Mr Barnsley is seated at an improvised desk on the dais, backing the empty throne and facing lines of empty benches. At his left elbow, Rev. Jones, perched on a cane chair is looking rather uncomfortable in the swirling smoke from Mr Barnsley's pipe. An armed guard stands behind them on the dais, two others man the two doors and Hezekiah waits languidly at the far corner.

Mr Barnsley: All right, Rev. Jones, you've got your brief recess—five minutes as you requested. Now, out with it, what's bothering you?

Rev. Jones: We need to reflect, sir. In the light of what you hinted me on the way here, you can see that there are just too many dark sides to your man. These are shocking and scandalous revelations coming from his people. I suggest you reconsider this move.

Mr Barnsley *[puffing at his pipe]*: Don't make a ghost, Rev. Jones. If I went changing my plans and programmes because of hearsay from the natives, we'd be long dead and dust.

Rev. Jones: But these allegations are too serious, sir. They are questions of character!

Mr Barnsley: Let me be quite blunt here. I don't need their opinions. All I owe anybody here is make them say something.

Rev. Jones: Of what practical use is that, sir?

Mr Barnsley: Oh, there's a Rule Book and it talks of consultation! Now, if you don't mind, can we get on?

Rev. Jones: Sir, if really we are just going through the motions, permit my say so, but not everyone appears taken as I'd been. The

Prime Minister and the royal lady, if you notice, haven't uttered a single word.

Mr Barnsley: The man is an old fox for sure, but his time is up. What do you think he has against my man?

Rev. Jones: In my opinion it's the whole kingdom that is opposed to your man, sir.

Mr Barnsley: That's what makes him the more the beast we need unleashed. He's going to be tough on them, which is what they deserve. No kid glove, no fake love. I will get all my taxes without much hassle. This is the first leg of my Project SAM and the Colonial Office has great expectations.

Rev. Jones: Project SAM?

Mr Barnsley: Yes Project SAM—That's for Shadrach, Abednego and Meshach, my programme for Ubulu, Umudimkpa and Umuachala. I trust you enjoy the significance of those bible names.

Rev. Jones: Shadrach, Meshach and Abednego were champions of faith, three holy youths who went through fire to prove our God to an unbelieving nation. Is that your mission for these ones, sir?

Mr Barnsley: We've had an interesting chat, Rev. Jones. *[Snapping his fingers]* Hezekiah, bring the people back!

[Hezekiah ushers in Akaeze, Oyidia and Orimili Obiora to a front bench and waits as Oche-ilo-eze, Echezo, Nnenna, Ugochi and others fill the other benches. Two armed guards push Mmanko in, in handcuffs, cursing, his eyes bloodshot. He is kept standing in the corner.]

Mmanko: Umudimkpa! Chei! Umudimkpa-a! It is not me they defeat. It is you!

Guard: Louder!

Hezekiah: Not Louder, say Order!

Mmanko: Akaeze, you are sitting there! Ah, fathers of my fore-fathers! Men are finished in this country!

Guard: Order!

Mr Barnsley: What is he saying, Hezekiah? Is he denying his part in the kidnap?

Hezekiah: I telling thee as I tolding thee before. He is not being agree to being answer that questions. He saying we and questions very useless foolish!

Mr Barnsley: That's interesting, but we need not waste much time with him. The missing girl was found tied up in his house and that speaks for itself. He goes to prison and that's a favour. Any comments, Rev. Jones?

Rev. Jones: None, sir.

Mr Barnsley: Where is the girl?

Hezekiah: She is being outside with others people of tie rope. Seven is them.

Mr Barnsley: Seven men tied like cattle at the back of the Chief Priest's house! I shudder, Rev. Jones. It would have been carnage tonight but for this timely visit and the excellent undercover work by my man, Abednego.

Rev. Jones: I hope all the ropes have been untied now, Hezekiah?

Hezekiah: Rope very wicked, tie too strong bad. Knife is using to being cutting the ropes for beautiful girl by her brothers with her father.

Mr Barnsley: Her father? That's the man on the bamboo bed—
interesting fellow! Bring them in.

[Exit Hezekiah]

Mmanko: Umudimkpa!

Guard: Louder! no. Order!

Mmanko: Akaeze, you are sitting there! Do you know your own is
coming? Hai! Umudimkpa-a-a-a!

Guard: Order!

Mmanko: Umudimkpa, ask of Ajofia! Ask what they have done to
your great son! Hai! Ajofia-a-a!

[Enter Abednego, beardless, a patch on the right eye]

Abednego: D.O. sir, let me for be answer this bad chief sharp, sharp. He
saying terrible to making trouble. I finish him for you.

Mr Barnsley: Yes, go ahead, Abednego. Go right ahead.

Abednego *[turns to Mmanko]*: Mmanko, did you hear the white man?
He said I can go and write on your head, if I want.

Mmanko: On my head!

Abednego: I advise you to just shut your mouth or bad things will
happen! Ajofia brought it on his own head and I was there
to see it. Nobody could touch him but nobody could save
him either. He said he would never give himself up. Instead,
he set his shrinehouse ablaze and walked into the fire. That
is the way he chose to die. You are different, Mmanko; you
won't get a choice.

Mmanko: What about your father? He will suffer double!

Abednego: My father is D.O. this great white man whose power brought you here like a chicken! He cannot suffer.

Mmanko: You are cursed!

Abednego: No, you blessed me only last night.

Mmanko: You were cursed by your own father!

Abednego: If you are talking of your old friend, the one they call Dikeogu, that one has disappeared. Ask the fighting men. They went with me to capture him as we captured you but Dikeogu turned into a falcon and just flew away. Why couldn't you do something like that for yourself?

Mmanko: Chei! Umudimkpa-a-a-a!

Guard: Order!

[Mr Barnsley nods, watching Abednego strut around]

Mr Barnsley *[to Rev. Jones]:* See how he takes charge. Very effective! Very confident!

[Re-enter Hezekiah, ushering in Uzoma. Her four brothers follow, bearing Iwobi on his bamboo bed. Uzoma is limping slightly. Nnenna her mother goes over and hugs her tightly]

Abednego: Iwobi! Sick man that made Death himself afraid! The man who offered his body to Death, and Death said Tufia!

[Iwobi, set down, lifts a hand. Umeji assists him to sit up]

Iwobi: Umudimkpa, join me in thanksgiving. Join me in thanksgiving. The gods have returned my voice and my strength; Uzo, my daughter is back alive too!

Mr Barnsley: What's he saying, Hezekiah?

Hezekiah: He telling thee thank you, thank you.

Abednego: He thanking God and thanking white man.

Mr Barnsley: Oh, this is touching, very touching. It just makes all that sacrifice worth the while.

Abednego: D.O. Sacrifice is them bush people and not you at all. Save is you and God.

Mr Barnsley: Tell you what? We shouldn't spoil this family's joy of reunion by keeping them waiting. Let them just go. Tell the man to go with his daughter and celebrate freedom. My issues are only with the so-called chiefs.

[Hezekiah begins but Abednego is quicker]

Abednego: Shhhh! D.O. is talking and I am the mouth that interpi for him. He says to you, Iwobi, go home with your people and dance. We found your daughter for you. You see how white man does his things?

Iwobi: Tell white man that I thank him. And I thank his brother even much more. But go home I will not because life without a good name is worse than death. White man must tell Umudimkpa the names of the people he said I tied up or I will die around his neck.

Abednego: If you know what is good for you, Iwobi, gather your bones now and get out of this place before white man changes his mind. Who is ant to stand in the way of the mighty elephant?

Mr Barnsley: What is he saying?

Hezekiah: He telling thee . . .

Abednego: D.O. is talking! Shut your mouth!

[Sergeant runs in]

Sergeant: Tell D.O. it is trouble! Big trouble! Them has killded policeman dead! Them has take him gun, take him uniform!

[General uproar . . . Fạde]

ACT 4, SCENE 5

Throne room at Umudimkpa palace. An angry Mr Barnsley is haranguing the glum Akaeze, Oyidia, Akaeze and a few others sitting on the wooden forms before him.

Abednego: White man is very kind. He is giving you the last chance to talk. Who killed police man? At my count of three . . . One! Two!

Mr Barnsley: Look, Abednego, tell these fools I could sack each and every one of them!

Abednego: White man says he can put all of you in a jute sack, like corn!

Mr Barnsley: In fact, I should fire them all.

Abednego: Chei, trouble! He says he will put you all in the fire!

Mr Barnsley: That's what I really should do. The die is cast.

Abednego: You see your trouble? He says you must die!

Mr Barnsley *[frustrated]*: Ask Rev. Jones to leave that sick man and get back here!

[Mr Barnsley retakes his seat, bristling]

Abednego: D.O. is talking. Police, call Rev. Jones here!

[Enter Sergeant, wailing]

Sergeant: Tell D.O. another two police o! Them has killded them dead o!

Abednego: What?

Sergeant: Another two policeman o! Ewe! Them take them gun, take them cloth o!

Mr Barnsley *[on his feet, shaking in rage]:* You idiot! What is your own job here? A reporter or policeman?

Sergeant *[shaking with fear]:* No sir! Yes sir!

Abednego: Aha!

Mr Barnsley: Bloody fool! You are losing men and guns out there and all you do is announce it to me!

Sergeant: No sir. Not nounce it. Only tolded you!

Mr Barnsley: What brainless apes! Gosh! I need a human being here! Where is Rev. Jones?

[Enter Rev. Jones and Hezekiah]

Mr Barnsley *[to Sergeant]:* Listen, you dumb oaf! You go out there and make arrests! Get me the blighters who killed your men! And I want those three guns back! Do you hear me? And don't you ever come back here to talk of more dead police men!

Sergeant: Shon sir! No complain'!

[Exit Sergeant]

Rev Jones: I'm really sorry to hear of these tragic deaths.

Mr Barnsley: I told you about the savage mentality of your natives. You thought it was a joke. What worries me now is guns in their hands.

Rev. Jones: If I may suggest, sir, let's engage their chiefs and elders with a bit more respect. There is real power in moral suasion.

Mr Barnsley *[gruffly]:* Please take your seat, Rev. Jones. I have an important announcement which is what brought me here.

[Rev. Jones gets seated. Mr Barnsley, pipe in mouth, opens a parchment on the desk]

Mr Barnsley: Bring in some of those outside; let as many as possible hear this direct from me. And while on that, confirm and reconfirm security!

[A general stir. More people are allowed in. They fill the seats; armed policemen stand on guard, and Mr Barnsley stands up]

Mr Barnsley: No administration worth its salt would allow the present state of anomie to continue.

Abednego: D.O. is talking. Everybody open your ears and hear him well. Anyone who makes noise here will be fined one goat and a bag of salt.

Mr Barnsley: What we have as leadership in this kingdom is a contraption that has past its time and relevance.

Abednego: Many many things are happening in this kingdom and people are suffering for nothing.

Mr Barnsley: It is a waning tyranny that has lost any pretension to credibility and influence.

Abednego: Very many bad things are happening and you are the people doing them and that cannot be tolerated by white man.

Mr Barnsley: We must stem the tide of wanton abductions and dastardly murders. We must restore law and order.

Abednego: Bastards and their mothers with those who want to support them must step to one side. We must rest on law and order.

Mr Barnsley: It is evident that the enfeebled regency holding sway in this palace cannot cope with the emergent challenges of taking this kingdom to its destiny in a new world of progress and distinction.

Abednego: Hezekiah, say that one.

Hezekiah: Hear O you people. White man says the world must progress.

Abednego: D.O. is talking. He says anyone who doesn't like progress, let him prepare to die. Umudimkpa must make progress!

Chorus: Ise-e!

Abednego: Umudimkpa must be head and never tail.

Chorus: Ise-e!

Mr Barnsley: Oh, they're excited to hear that. *[To Rev. Jones]* The regime is even more unpopular than I reckoned. Well, this should smoothen things. Get up here, Abednego.

[Commotion outside. Enter Sergeant and two policemen pushing Egbuna in, his wrists and ankles tied]

Egbuna: Amadiora will break your heads! You sons of pigs that feed on white vomit. May Agbala burst your entrails and pluck your testicles!

Constable: Order!

Sergeant: Shon sir! We arrest sir! Bad boy son of wicked chief Ajofia, juju man of burn fire die !

Mr Barnsley: Is he the one that killed the police men?

Sergeant: Yes sir! Shon sir!

Egbuna: Oyidi'a, High Mother, what are the tears for? The beatings they rain on my body are a joy to my spirit! Ajofia my father has gone in the pride of a true warrior. I will not let him down by dropping a tear . . .

Constable: Order!

Abednego: Foolish boy! You want to die like your father! Stubborn goat!

Egbuna: You are the dog they call Apiti. I am coming to get you even when I die. By the gods, I will wipe that smile off your face.

Constable: Order!

Abednego: D.O. sir, he bad head of juju, like his father.

Mr Barnsley: Take him away! Arrest all the others and recover the guns!

Sergeant: Yes sir! Shon sir! No complain'!

[Sergeant and his men push the struggling Egbuna towards the exit]

Egbuna: Leave me alone you bastards! Pigs and puddle-toads! You will die all of you! I will kill you! Kill you!

Constable: Order!

[Exeunt]

Mr Barnsley: Step forward, Abednego. Yes, on the dais. Good. Now face the people.

Mr Barnsley: My good people of Umudimkpa . . .

Abednego: D.O. is talking. He says . . . .

Mr Barnsley: This is about you, Abednego. *[Stands beside him]* Hezekiah will interprete.

Mr Barnsley: It is my great pleasure today to present to you one of our own.

Hezekiah: D.O. is telling you, this is your own countryman.

Mr Barnsley: The very best of you.

Hezekiah: He is good for you.

Mr Barnsley: He will represent me to you and represent you to me.

Hezekiah: He will work for me and help you.

Abednego: Say correct! Say correct. D.O. is talking of presents—all presents. He says you will give me any present you want to give him and if he has any present for you, he will give them to me for you.

Mr Barnsley: It is a position of the highest trust. He has authority as king.

Hezekiah: He is higher than all chiefs. He is like king.

Mr Barnsley: He is to be known as Paramount Ruler. This means he is the highest traditional authority in this place. He is the face of Government and he will collect taxes for the Government. The police will be placed under him and he will sit in judgment over your matters.

Abednego: D.O. is talking. Tell them all he has said. Very important!

Hezekiah: He is given all powers of Government. Police and court will work under him and everybody must obey him.

Abednego: Say complete! I didn't hear tax!

Hezekiah: He will collect tax too.

Mr Barnsley: It is a great day for Umudimkpa. You must thank heavens that it is one of your own that is chosen to occupy this exalted office. *[Standing beside Abednego, he grips his arm and raises it high]* By the powers in me vested as the Acting District Officer of the Ubulu Native Administrative Area, I present to you the Paramount Ruler Of all Umudimkpa—your man, Abednego!

Rev. Jones: The people are not looking pleased or excited. But I suppose congratulations are in order?

Mr Barnsley: Yes, you may congratulate him. Everybody should congratulate him.

Rev. Jones *[icily]*: Well then, congratulations.

Mr Barnsley *[shaking hands warmly with Abednego]*: Congratulation.

Abednego: Thank you sir, thank you very much, my D.O. But what can am I say now? Are you true true or joke joke? Can am I be king for true?

Mr Barnsley: You are king, Abednego. Full king. Paramount Ruler.

Abednego: They think is joke joke!

Mr Barnsley: Command anyone anything!

Abednego: Command you?

Mr Barnsley: Yes, even me.

Abednego: Give me smoke pipe!

[Mr Barnsley shrugs but removes the pipe in his mouth and hands it to him. Abednego laughing excitedly, puts it to his lips and puffs]

Mr Barnsley: Hail King Abednego.

Abednego: Good, good. D.O. see eh? Give me your ride chair.

Mr Barnsley: It's yours, O king. Command them to bring it.

Abednego: Hezekiah! This your name is too long! Tell them to bring the riding chair! Did you not hear D.O.? I am king.

[At a signal from Hezekiah, the four porters trot in and set down the sedan. Abednego mounts, puffing at his pipe, and they lift up]

Rev. Jones: Not a word to his subjects before he leaves?

Mr Barnsley: Yes, king, I suggest you say a few words. Maybe about paying taxes.

Abednego: Very important, very important. *[To the porters]* Lower the chair . . . I did not say put it down! Always listen well when I talk! I am King of Umudimkpa. White man said it!

[The porters squat, bearing him up]

Abednego: Umudimkpa, I must tell you that you have not started well. White man himself has made me the king but instead of rejoicing with me, your faces are tight like donkeys. Do you prefer a stranger to come and rule us? Is that what you want? I am ready for anybody's fight. I have the police and we have the guns. In your own interest, just accept that the past is past; the future has started today. There will be no more undeserved privileges for people like Obiora Orimili. He expects the whole world to fall at his feet because he is married to Ugochi, princess of Umuachala. All that nonsense is over. I am going to bring development here. I will build a befitting prison for you, so there will be no need to send people all the way to Ubulu or Onicha. White man has told you about tax. Anyone of you who does not want big trouble must pay big tax. One thing very important to white man is tax; so we shall give him more than he is asking for. I will talk to you better at my coronation when I wear the kind of clothes and a cap that suits a paramount ruler.

[A shot rings out. There is instant pandemonium, the porters dropping their human cargo in panic. Mr Barnley flees unceremoniously as Egbuna bursts in, trailing partially loosened ropes from his wrists and ankles, a smoking gun in his trembling hands.]

Constable: Give me my gun! Give me my gun! Aah!

Egbuna: I hope I've killed that bastard!

[Egbuna is quickly overpowered. Abednego, cowering on the floor, picks himself up. Rev Jones is sprawled out on the dais, a crimson patch spreading on the front of his white soutane. Pregnant woman wails a heart-rending lament.]

Hezekiah *[to Egbuna]*: See what you have done.

The End.